Standing Up to OCD
Workbook for Kids

STANDING UP to OCD

WORKBOOK for KIDS

40 Activities to Help Children Stop
Unwanted Thoughts, Control Compulsive
Behaviors, and Overcome Anxiety

TYSON REUTER, PHD

ILLUSTRATED BY SARAH REBAR

callisto
publishing
an imprint of Sourcebooks

Copyright © 2019 by Callisto Publishing LLC
Cover and internal design © 2019 by Callisto Publishing LLC
Illustrations © 2019 Sarah Rebar
Cover Designer: Joshua Moore
Interior Designer: Erik Jacobsen
Art Manager: Michael Hardgrove
Editors: Daniel Grogan, Sean Newcott
Production Editor: Erum Khan

Callisto Kids and the colophon are registered trademarks of Callisto Publishing LLC.

All rights reserved. No part of this book may be reproduced in any form or by any electronic or mechanical means including information storage and retrieval systems—except in the case of brief quotations embodied in critical articles or reviews—without permission in writing from its publisher, Sourcebooks LLC.

All brand names and product names used in this book are trademarks, registered trademarks, or trade names of their respective holders. Callisto Publishing is not associated with any product or vendor in this book.

Published by Callisto Publishing LLC C/O Sourcebooks LLC
P.O. Box 4410, Naperville, Illinois 60567-4410
(630) 961-3900
callistopublishing.com

This product conforms to all applicable CPSC and CPSIA standards.

Source of Production: Wing King Tong Paper Products Co.Ltd. Shenzhen, Guangdong Province, China
Date of Production: October 2023
Run Number: 5035321

Printed and bound in China
WKT 2

CONTENTS

INTRODUCTION FOR
PARENTS

Before you and your child begins working through this book, it's important to understand a little more about OCD so you can be most supportive and helpful. For child-oriented content, flip to page 13.

Just over three decades ago, *obsessive-compulsive disorder* (OCD) was considered untreatable, puzzling clinicians, researchers, parents, and patients alike. Thankfully, those times are behind us. These last 30 to 40 years have brought about significant advances in behavioral and pharmacological treatments that have changed the way we see OCD.

However, without treatment, OCD can remain every bit as difficult as it is debilitating. Whether recently diagnosed or not, seeing your child suffer can be extremely distressing. Perhaps you're feeling hopeless or confused. Maybe you've fallen into the trap of saying, "Just stop," or "Why do you keep doing that?"

But there is hope. With the correct type of therapy and hard work, OCD is quite treatable. Although the term isn't used, the entire backbone that weaves this workbook together is based on *cognitive behavioral therapy*, or CBT for short. In a nutshell, CBT is an empirically supported treatment that has been scientifically proven to treat OCD, with extremely promising results.

In fact, CBT has been shown to reduce symptoms as effectively as, and sometimes more effectively than, medication. This is not to say medications are unhelpful. Indeed, sometimes they are warranted, and the combination of medication and therapy is necessary at times. But the point is that with the combination of consistent practice and targeted therapy, OCD is treatable. People can and do get better.

Cognitive Behavioral Therapy 101

CBT is a psychotherapy that assumes our emotions, thoughts, and behaviors are connected and influence one other. With OCD, your child may feel extremely anxious. But telling your child not to feel anxious doesn't work. It doesn't make your child feel any less worried, and oftentimes, it just makes them feel worse.

Think of the last time you were angry and someone asked you to calm down, or the last time you were sad and someone told you to cheer up. It doesn't work! If it were that easy, I wouldn't have a career as a psychologist. I would just tell my patients in the first session to not feel anxious and not have OCD—and they'd be cured!

Put simply, we can't change the way we feel just by choosing to feel differently. Similarly, your child cannot simply choose to not feel anxious. However, we can change the way we think, and we can change the way we behave. And because thoughts and behaviors are related to our emotions, we can therefore target how we feel.

OCD consists of two parts: obsessions and compulsions. Obsessions are thoughts. Compulsions are behaviors. And we have the power to change both.

Obsessive-Compulsive Disorder 101

Obsessions are intrusive, unwanted thoughts or images that can cause significant distress and anxiety. These thoughts can be about contamination, unwanted sexual thoughts or images, fear of harming themselves or others, religious preoccupations, and many others. Because these thoughts are so unpleasant, it's no surprise that your child tries to ignore, push away, or "neutralize" them.

This is where compulsions come in. Compulsions are repetitive behaviors or acts, done out in the open or mentally, that your child feels they need to do in order to prevent some feared outcome. These rituals are often done a specific way, a certain number of times, or until it feels "just right."

The central purpose of compulsions is to reduce anxiety. Compulsions do not have to be connected to the obsessions in a realistic or logical manner. For example, a child might have to slam a car door three times in order to get rid of an unwanted sexual thought. Importantly, kids may not be able to articulate why they engage in their compulsions. For some kids, they may not see them as excessive or disconnected from their obsessions.

As you help your child through this workbook, they'll learn how to become an expert in their OCD. They'll learn to identify their obsessions and compulsions and know when it's their OCD talking. They'll also learn strategies grounded in CBT to help them observe, challenge, and ultimately change their thinking. They'll learn how to slowly confront their fears, starting with the easiest, and work their way up to the more challenging fears.

At the same time, they'll learn how to resist their compulsions. This is called *exposure and response prevention*, or ERP for short.

A good rule of thumb is that OCD, like all anxiety, often makes children overestimate their fears and underestimate their ability to handle these fears. Through repeated practice, your child learns to think about things realistically. Instead of overestimating their fears, they'll learn that things aren't quite as bad as they expected. Instead of underestimating their ability to handle these fears, they'll learn that they're better able to cope than they thought.

What Makes Treatment Successful?

Success in therapy boils down to three things: hard work, targeted interventions, and strong therapeutic alliance.

Hard work: Just like eating one salad doesn't make you lose weight, resisting one compulsion one time does not lead to meaningful and lasting change. It can take just one trial to learn fear; it can take hundreds of trials to unlearn it. Therefore, it's extremely important that you encourage your child to keep practicing.

OCD treatment is very hard work, especially in the beginning. However, as your child continues to practice, it gets easier and easier. Things that they once thought were extremely distressing become less difficult. Keep it up!

Targeted interventions: To treat OCD, you need a certain type of psychotherapy. CBT is an empirically supported treatment that has been scientifically proven to treat OCD. Hypnosis, psychoanalysis, and supportive therapy just don't cut it—at least not for OCD. Put bluntly: Some psychotherapies for OCD work. Others don't.

Strong alliance: The single most important factor in seeing improvement is something called therapeutic alliance. This is the strength of the relationship between the child and therapist. This isn't to say, however, that your child cannot see improvement without working with a therapist.

But if you or your child are finding it difficult to stay motivated and practice the exercises in this workbook, consider incorporating professional help. Given that OCD is nuanced and responds best to a specific type of therapy, it's strongly recommended to work with a clinician who has experience and expertise in evidence-based treatments.

If you choose to work with a mental health professional, look for buzzwords like "cognitive behavioral therapy (CBT)," "exposure and response prevention (ERP)," or "acceptance and commitment therapy (ACT)." For help finding a clinician and additional resources on OCD, look to the end of this workbook.

How You Can Help

Seeing your child get upset by intrusive thoughts and "stuck" in seemingly never-ending patterns of rechecking, redoing, rewashing, and recounting is incredibly hard as a parent. But there are many things you can do—and a few things you shouldn't do—that'll help you be the most supportive, loving, and effective while helping your child stand up to their OCD. Here are a few key points to keep in mind.

This is really hard. While it may seem like only washing your hands for 15 seconds and walking away is effortless, for a child with OCD, this can be extremely difficult. For an outside observer, it may seem like your child should just know that, by now, their hands are certainly clean. But for your child, this can be a very painful, vicious cycle of washing, doubting, and anxiety.

It's a nightmare that just doesn't seem to end.

If you could peek inside your child's brain, they could be replaying in their mind, "I think my hands are clean, but what if they're not? I better wash one more time—just in case. Oops, I didn't do it correctly that time. I need to start all over. Now my dad is yelling at me. I need to stop, or I'll get in trouble. I can't stand this. I can't stop. Why can't I just stop?! What's wrong with me?!"

It goes without saying, but try to remain patient and supportive. If your child gets down on themselves, like in the example above, immediately correct them in a kind manner: "Nothing is wrong with you. I can't imagine how difficult this is, but I know you can do it."

Sometimes it gets worse before it gets better. This may sound counterintuitive. But the way your child has been managing their obsessions is to engage in their compulsions. Remember, these serve to reduce their anxiety. And the way we treat OCD is to help your child resist their compulsions.

For example, if your child has a distressing thought, they may neutralize this by, say, checking the refrigerator door over and over again. With treatment, eventually your child learns that nothing bad happens when they don't check the refrigerator. They learn that their distressing thought has no power and their feared outcome was wrong.

However, until then, we're asking them to resist doing the *very thing* that they've learned will reduce their anxiety. We're stripping away the action that, in their mind, is the only way to make their obsession go away and make them feel better. But again, over time and with continued practice, your child will learn that this is not the case.

Try not to accommodate. This is where I see parents and caregivers struggle the most. Suppose your child has an intrusive thought that they're unclean and will contaminate you because they just gave you a hug. Your child revs up to high anxiety and repeatedly seeks reassurance: "Did I get you sick? Are you okay? Mommy, are you sure? Are you going to die?"

As a parent, you don't want to see your child in distress. So, you understandably respond, "Of course not, I'm just fine. No need to worry!"

A predictable pattern happens here that inadvertently accommodates the anxiety. First, your child continues an onslaught of reassurance-seeking questions. You, a loving parent, see your child in distress as their anxiety continues to build. This is very hard to tolerate, especially when the real answers to your child's questions seem so obvious: "Of course, I'm just fine!" You want to do everything you can to help your child feel better, so you reassure them that everything is fine. Immediately, you seem to take away your child's anxiety by reassuring them, and you see a wave of calmness wash over them.

Although very well intended, this chain of events isn't helping your child in the long run. Reassurance for OCD leads to an increasing loop of frustration for both you and your child: "Yes, yes, I'm okay! How many times do I have to tell you?!" Keep in mind that reassurance seeking is often a compulsion. And the goal of successfully standing up to OCD is helping your child resist compulsions, not give in to them.

Although certainly not your intent, by providing reassurance, your child has given more power to their thoughts. They've strengthened the belief that *thinking* about something terrible happening means that something terrible *will* happen.

So, if your child asks you to participate in one of their compulsions, instead of providing reassurance, sometimes a couple of good lines to use are, "This is your OCD talking. Let's just see what happens if we don't [insert compulsion]." At that point, you could even start a timer and praise your child: "Wow! You went a whole two minutes without [insert compulsion]. Great job!" Next time, you shoot for resisting a little longer.

Remember, the ultimate goal of OCD treatment can be summarized as this: Your child repeatedly resists the things OCD tells them they need to do until they learn that their thoughts, worries, and fears were wrong. And that is how learning occurs and progress is made: learning you were wrong.

How to Make a Reward Chart

To help your child stay motivated, it often helps to set up an incentive system. It'll be reasonable and fair for both of you. Having some rewards in place can keep the ball rolling and encourage your child to continue to practice!

There are many ways to set this up. Here are a few ground rules.

Be specific. The more specific the goal, the better. You may have heard of SMART goals. SMART stands for Specific, Measurable, Attainable, Relevant, and Timely. For example, setting a goal of, "I want to get in shape," is not as likely to be accomplished as a goal of, "I'm going to run outside for 20 minutes after dinner every Monday, Wednesday, and Friday."

The same is true for standing up to OCD. For example, an unhelpful goal would be, "Get better at not washing so much." What exactly does "better" mean? And how do you define "not washing"? Does that include showering? Or only hands? What about hand sanitizer—is that still okay? Are we talking five seconds or five minutes?

Instead, a better goal would be, "I'm only going to wash my hands after using the bathroom and before meals. I'll set a timer and give myself no more than 15 seconds. When the timer is done, I leave the bathroom/kitchen."

The more immediate the reward, the better. Try to keep the rewards in the near future. Just like looking forward to having a fun night with friends this weekend might get you through a difficult week more than a vacation the following summer will, your child is likely more motivated to work harder to go to their favorite ice cream store this week than a trip to Disney World next year.

Be fair and consistent, but flexible if needed. A $5 gift card shouldn't take half a day to earn, but it also shouldn't take half a year. Also, if you find that your child is racking up points or rewards too slowly—or too quickly—it's fine to adjust. Just be sure to follow through.

If you agree your daughter can cash in 10 points for 10 extra minutes of screen time, and she worked for those points fairly, then she should be given that reward. If you suddenly or randomly change the rules, this will de-motivate and dis-incentivize. Imagine if you went to work next week and your boss decided to not pay you that week—just because.

Finally, no taking away points. If your daughter earned them, they're hers. Even if she was being rude to her brother in the car ride to school this morning. Think of a different consequence that's separate from working on OCD.

Mix it up. Use a combination of small, medium, and large rewards. Similarly, doing more difficult things should earn more points than doing things that are easy.

But remember, determining what's hard or easy may be subjective to your child. To them, resisting checking that the front door is locked may be easier than resisting checking that their school binder is zipped closed. The "rules" of OCD are often not logical, so don't expect what your child deems as difficult or easy to necessarily make sense objectively.

Do not punish. Above all, never punish your child for their OCD. One, it doesn't work. We know very clearly from tons of research that praising a desirable behavior is more effective than punishing an undesirable one. Two, it just makes your child feel worse. They're probably already disappointed in themselves.

So, if they were unable to, say, go to bed without rearranging their toys or checking under their bed five times, just validate that this is really hard, reiterate you know they can do it, and encourage them to try again next time.

Some parents use tickets. Others use marbles. Or you can use a point system. For example, say your child struggles with opening and closing the kitchen drawers. Suppose they have to open and close them in multiples of threes. If your child is able to open and close a drawer just once and resist the urge to open and close it two more times, they should receive a point.

Another example: Say your child needs to have the blanket on their bed folded "just so." If they are able to fold it "wrong" and sit with the uncomfortable feeling, they should receive a point.

On page 9 is an example chart, and there are two blank templates on page 10, but feel free to use whatever system works best for you and your child.

THINGS I CAN DO TO EARN POINTS	EARNS
Check that the door is locked once and walk away	1
Go 30 minutes without asking my parents if I will get sick	3
Open all doors in the house on my own for 1 hour	5
Touch a "germy" doorknob, give my parent a hug, and not ask them if they're okay	3

THINGS I CAN SPEND MY POINTS ON	COSTS
Ten extra minutes of screen time on a weekday	15
Get $2 of in-app purchases for my video game	25
Go to my favorite ice cream store	70
Have a sleepover with my best friend	100

THINGS I CAN DO TO EARN POINTS	EARNS

THINGS I CAN SPEND MY POINTS ON	COSTS

Final Thoughts

It can be extremely upsetting to see your child suffer. Watching them repeat, count, check, wash, pray, doubt, rearrange, order, and be plagued by "what if" thoughts can be stressful for everyone.

But there is hope. Remember, OCD is treatable. It just takes hard work, practice, and unconditional support. Whether your child is already working with a therapist or this is your first time learning about OCD, congratulations on taking a step toward helping your child stand up to their OCD. It's my hope that you and your child will learn coping skills and strategies to use every step of the way, no matter where their journey takes them.

INTRODUCTION FOR
KIDS

Being a kid can be hard. Having OCD can make things even harder. With OCD, even everyday things can be difficult. Some kids with OCD feel very anxious. OCD causes some kids to have scary thoughts that don't always make sense and seem to come out of nowhere. Some kids with OCD have to check things again and again no matter how hard they try to stop. OCD can also make some kids say or do something a certain way until it feels "just right."

OCD can make you feel "stuck."

But you're not alone! Many kids struggle with OCD. Having OCD doesn't mean you're "crazy" or "weird." And you didn't cause your OCD.

In this workbook, you and your family are going to learn ways to stand up to OCD by creating an OCD toolbox. Just like a car mechanic uses tools to fix a car, you'll learn about many tools you can add to your toolbox to help you feel better.

Just like a detective, you'll learn how to spot your OCD thoughts. You'll learn how to take charge and say no to OCD. You'll learn how to be brave and slowly face the things OCD tells you are scary. And you'll learn skills that you can use anywhere to help you feel less worried.

Think of an activity you're really good at. Maybe you're great at baseball or playing the piano. Maybe you're a video game champion. What would happen if you practiced this activity just a few minutes a week? Would you get any better? Of course not! To get better at something, we need to practice. After all, practice makes perfect.

The same is true for standing up to OCD. It'll be very important for you to keep practicing the activities you learn in this book. The good news is, the more you practice, the more tools you'll have in your toolbox. The more tools you have, the easier it will be to stand up to OCD. It'll take time, but it'll get easier. And you'll start to feel better.

Great job taking the first step to standing up to your OCD. Your hard work is going to pay off. Remember, you can do this!

CHAPTER 1

WHAT DOES OCD MEAN TO ME?

Do you ever count things a certain number of times and feel like you just can't stop? Or maybe you worry about germs and think you need to wash your hands over and over again? Do you rearrange your toys until it feels "just right"? Do scary thoughts ever get "stuck" in your head and keep bothering you?

These thoughts, feelings, and actions are called OCD, which stands for *obsessive-compulsive disorder*. With OCD, even everyday things can be very difficult. But you need to know that you're not alone. And there is nothing wrong with you as a person. It's your OCD talking, and you're going to learn to stand up to it so you can go on living your life as a happy, healthy kid.

Feeling "Stuck"

Feeling "stuck" is a frustrating feeling. With OCD, kids often feel "stuck" on many things many times throughout the day. This feeling can be different for everyone. Let's look at a story about Isabella.

ISABELLA'S STORY

Isabella is eight years old and has OCD. After a long, busy day at school, she starts to get ready for bed. After brushing her teeth and using the bathroom, she washes her hands. She takes two pumps of soap and turns the faucet on and off twice. She rubs her hands together with warm, soapy water.

After a few seconds, she stops but worries, "What if they're not clean?" So, she takes two more pumps of soap: "One, two," she says out loud. And two more times she turns the faucet: "One, two." Isabella washes her hands over and over and just can't seem to stop. She worries, "If I don't keep washing, then I'll get really sick."

A few minutes go by and Isabella is still washing and worrying. Her mom knocks on the door asking if she's finished and telling her to go to bed. Isabella asks, "Are you sure my hands are clean? What if I get sick?" Her mom tells her that everything's fine and she won't get sick. Right away, Isabella feels better.

But the feeling doesn't last long. She starts to walk to her bed, counting her steps. The steps have to land on an even number before she hops into bed. She takes her left foot and counts to herself, "One . . ." Now right foot. "Two . . ." Left foot. "Three . . ." She counts and walks and counts and walks to bed and ends on, "nine."

Uh-oh. Something feels wrong. She tries to get into bed, but it just doesn't feel right. It needs to be an even number. Feeling frustrated, Isabella walks back to the bathroom and starts over.

GETTING UNSTUCK

Does Isabella's story remind you of yourself? What are some things she gets "stuck" on? Now, what are some things you get "stuck" on? Write down the things that OCD tells you to do to make yourself feel better.

What Is OCD?

Let's take another look at Isabella's story. Kids who don't have OCD can wash their hands just once. They can easily step away from the sink and go on with their bedtime routine.

But not Isabella. She has to do things a certain number of times. She needs to take two pumps of soap and turn the faucet on and off twice. She finds it hard to stop her worries and thoughts. She knows that her hands are clean, but she still needs to ask her mother to make sure—just in case. She counts her steps and can't go to bed unless she stops on an even number. If she doesn't, she needs to start all over again until it feels "just right."

Isabella has OCD.

The "**O**" stands for *obsessions*. Obsessions are unwanted thoughts or images that come into your head that you just can't make go away.

Sometimes the thoughts are scary. Sometimes they make no sense. No matter how hard you try to push them away or stop thinking about them, it feels like you can't. They just keep bothering you. And this makes you even more worried.

For Isabella, the thought that won't go away is that her hands aren't clean. She just can't stop thinking about how she might get sick.

The "**C**" stands for *compulsions*. Compulsions are actions you feel you have to do.

The action can be out in the open, like washing your hands, tapping or touching things a certain number of times, putting things in order, redoing your homework, or asking your parent, "Are you sure?" again and again. Or the action can be in your head, like praying, counting, checking, or repeating certain numbers or words.

Whatever it is, you do the action over and over again. It isn't something you enjoy doing or even want to do. It's OCD telling you things you have to do to make the thought go away so you can feel less worried.

For Isabella, the actions she has to do are washing her hands and counting her steps a certain way. She has "rules" in her mind that she has to follow. If she doesn't follow these "rules," she gets more worried and has to start all over.

The "**D**" stands for *disorder*. A disorder is an unusual way of thinking or behaving that causes stress and worry and makes everyday life more difficult. OCD is a type of anxiety disorder. Anxiety is another word for worry.

THOUGHTS AND FEELINGS

Imagine that the kid below is you. See the little thought bubble above their head? In that bubble, write down one of your thoughts that you just can't stop thinking about, no matter how hard you try.

Now notice all the feelings around their head, like "sad" or "worried" or "frustrated." When this thought pops in your head, how does it make you feel? Circle all the feelings that you have when you get this thought.

What sort of things do you do to make that thought go away? Are there any "rules" you have to follow?

FRUSTRATED

WORRIED

SAD   EMBARRASSED

GUILTY   SCARED

How Does OCD Work?

At first, OCD might start with having thoughts that are scary or don't make sense. These thoughts are usually about bad things happening to you or other people. Even more terrible is that these thoughts seem to come out of nowhere. No one likes having bad thoughts, especially if they seem to pop into your head without warning. So, you try to make them go away.

Remember compulsions? These are the things you do or say to make the thoughts leave you alone. You do your compulsions to feel less worried.

This might be washing your hands over and over, like Isabella. It could be arranging stuff a certain way. It might be checking or counting things. It could be repeating the same thing over and over. It could be asking your friend a question you already know the answer to. It might be making things feel even or doing something until it feels just right. It could be writing, erasing, and rewriting your homework again and again.

Most of the time, you *know* in your head that what you're doing doesn't make any sense. But with OCD, it doesn't matter if the action doesn't make sense. There's always a "what if" in your head. You just can't seem to stop until things are "just right" or you have "made sure." You have to keep doing or saying things until you get that feeling that says, "Ahh, that feels better. Now I can stop."

For a while, you might feel less nervous. But the feeling doesn't last long. OCD usually makes you doubt yourself—and you start all over again. And the cycle goes on and on. It's so hard and so frustrating! Sometimes it makes you feel sad or angry or even more worried.

You might be asking yourself, "How do I stop the cycle?" That's a great question! In this workbook, you're going to learn many tools to stop OCD from repeating itself on an endless loop. You'll learn to talk back to your thoughts and how to stop yourself from doing the things OCD is telling you that you have to do.

WHAT DOES YOUR OCD LOOP LOOK LIKE?

In the space below, write down one of your obsessions. Remember, an obsession is a thought that pops into your head that you don't want and can't seem to stop thinking about.

Next, write down one of your compulsions. Remember, a compulsion is something you do or say over and over again that your OCD tells you that you need to do. Your compulsion is the thing you do to make you feel better and less worried or scared.

Connect your obsession and compulsion with an arrow. Which direction does the arrow go in? Does it go just one way? Or does it go back and forth? Most of the time, you have an obsession, which makes you feel more worried. This makes you do your compulsion, which makes you feel less worried.

Why Does OCD Happen?

Have you ever used flour to bake something? Sometimes, you have to sift the flour before you add it to the bowl. As you gently tap the sifter, the clumps of flour get smaller and smaller until they pass through the tiny holes of the sifter.

Our brains are just like sifters—and there are so many things that they have to deal with! Every second, we see colors, hear sounds, feel textures, and have thoughts. Most of the time, our brains can sift all of these things with no problem. But with OCD, sometimes thoughts that should go through the "brain sifter" *don't* go through. Just like a lump of flour might get stuck, sometimes thoughts get "stuck" in our brain—and our brain won't let them pass through.

Let's say one of your morning chores is to feed the dog. Right before heading off to school, you get a big scoop of dog food and drop it into your furry friend's bowl—plop! Now it's time for school. You get in the car with your parent and off you go.

You're in the car for only two minutes, but all of a sudden you have a thought: "Did I feed the dog?" In your mind, you try to see the image of yourself feeding the dog. You can see your hand go into the dog food bag and scoop the food. You can picture your puppy wagging her tail looking so excited. You can even hear the "plop" as the food fills up the bowl. You can see yourself feeding your dog so clearly just a few minutes ago. You know you fed your dog . . . right?

But OCD makes you think, "What if I didn't? What if I forgot? I should go back and check—just in case."

With OCD, even though you can replay the memory of feeding your dog in your mind, you still can't help thinking, "What if I didn't? What if

I forgot?" Then your OCD might bring up even more worries: "What if something bad happens, like she gets hungry and sick?" Now your brain gets "stuck" on this bad thought. Your brain doesn't let it pass through the sifter. It doesn't let you accept the fact that you did feed your dog. The thought of your dog getting hungry and sick is bad. In your mind, going back to check to make sure you fed her makes sense.

But here's something very important to remember: Having the thought of something happening is different from something actually happening in real life. Just because you think about something in your mind, it doesn't mean it'll come true in real life.

For example, let's say you're playing baseball. You're up to bat. Let's say you think about hitting a home run. You think *really, really* hard about hitting a home run. You hear the loud crack of the bat. You imagine the ball soaring through the air like a bird. You can see your teammates cheering you on as you sprint around the bases. You feel so happy and excited!

Now, does thinking about hitting a home run—even if you think really, really hard about it—mean that you will actually hit a home run? Do the thoughts in your mind, just by themselves, have the power to make a home run happen?

The home run example shows how thinking about something is very different from something happening for real. The same is true when OCD tells you bad thoughts. OCD can make you think of terrible things that might happen. OCD can make you see very scary images that you don't want to see.

But remember: You can *think* of something awful happening—like your dog getting sick—but that doesn't mean it will happen.

Let's put it another way: Thoughts are just thoughts. *Thoughts are not facts*. And a lot of the time, thoughts are not true at all.

SIFTING FLOUR

Remember how we talked about our brains being like sifters? Just like flour sometimes gets stuck in a sifter, sometimes with OCD you get "stuck."

Below is a picture of a giant sifter and a giant bag of flour. Most of the flour is getting through, but some is getting stuck. How do we get stuck flour through a sifter? We tap the sifter!

Now, can you think of a real-life example of when your OCD makes you feel "stuck"? Next to the sifter, draw some ways OCD makes you feel "stuck."

Is It OCD?

We all get worried sometimes. In fact, a little bit of anxiety can be a good thing. For example, let's say you have a big test tomorrow. What would happen if you didn't have any anxiety? Would you take the time to prepare for the test? Would you study?

Probably not. If you had no anxiety at all, you might say to yourself, "I've got this. It'll be so easy. I don't even need to go over my notes at all. I'm 100% positive I'll get an A+."

While being positive and confident is a good thing, a little bit of anxiety can actually help us solve problems. It gets our brains ready. In this case, some anxiety might make you prepare for your big test and study. And this will lead to something good: You'll probably get a better grade than if you didn't study.

But a little bit of anxiety and OCD are two very different things. Let's look at two stories that will help you learn the difference. First, let's hear Xavier's story. Then we'll take a look at Karen's story.

XAVIER'S STORY

Xavier is eight years old and in the second grade. He's learning about planets in science class. The teacher tells the class they have a quiz tomorrow on naming all of the planets. Xavier feels a little nervous. He thinks to himself, "What if I don't do well tomorrow? What if I fail the quiz? I should probably study so that I do well."

That night, Xavier unzips his backpack, takes out his binder, and decides to study. He has all his classes labeled neatly. He flips to the divider labeled "science" and starts reading his list of planets. "Mercury . . . Venus . . . Earth . . ." He keeps studying his list until he feels he knows it. Now that he feels prepared for the quiz, Xavier feels less nervous. He puts his binder down and gets ready for bed.

KAREN'S STORY

Karen is also eight years old and in the second grade. She's in Xavier's class and was also told there will be a quiz tomorrow. She feels nervous and worries that she won't do well. She decides to start studying. She unzips her backpack, but for some reason, once just doesn't feel like enough. So, she zips and unzips her backpack over and over again until the zippers clink together to make a certain sound.

Karen then takes out her binder, which is also labeled neatly with all of her classes. She sees the divider labeled "science" and spells out the word in her head: "S . . . c . . . i . . . e . . . n . . . c . . . e." But she can't stop. Something feels "off." So, she spells the word "science" a few more times.

She pulls out her list of planets and starts to memorize them. "Mercury . . . Venus . . . Earth . . ." But something doesn't feel right. She has to start over. "No wait . . . Mercury." She points to the planet, rereads it, and taps twice. "Then Venus." Reread. Two taps. "Earth." Reread. Two taps.

Karen starts to get frustrated. Twenty minutes have already gone by. She wants to stop, but she just can't. She needs to do certain things in a certain order.

KAREN AND XAVIER

Which story sounds like worry, and which story sounds like OCD? What are the differences? Think about a situation when you're a little worried versus when OCD is taking over. How can you tell the difference? Remember, sometimes a little bit of worry can be a good thing. If you worry about a test in school then it might lead you to study hard and be more prepared. OCD causes you to worry in a bad way. That is why we always want to be on the lookout for OCD thoughts. Write down your thoughts on the lines.

How Do I Beat OCD?

Remember the description of how our brains act like a sifter? With OCD, thoughts that would normally pass through the sifter sometimes don't. This can make you feel frustrated and worried. OCD makes you think things like "what if" and "just in case" and "make sure."

Sometimes OCD will make you have scary thoughts that won't leave you alone. You worry about the worst thing in the world happening. To make these thoughts go away, you give in to your OCD. You listen to it. If OCD tells you that you need to go back and check something, you do it. If OCD tells you that you have to wash your hands again and again, you do it. And if OCD tells you that you must count objects over and over, you do it.

OCD is like a big, hungry monster. Every time you listen to your OCD to check or repeat something—or tell yourself "just in case"—you're feeding the monster. When you keep feeding that monster, it gets stronger and stronger. And that monster just gets hungrier and hungrier. It keeps wanting more. That monster just never seems to get full!

But there's no need to worry. Right now, it might seem like your OCD has all the power. That can feel really scary. The good news is there are many tools you can learn that will help you stop feeding that hungry monster and stand up to your OCD.

First, there are three things about us that are important to understand: thoughts, feelings, and actions.

Thoughts: These are the things we think of. They can be exciting, like, "I can't wait for summer!" They can be scary, like, "I'm worried that bee is going to sting me!" Or they can also be a simple fact, like, "Green is a color."

Feelings: These are emotions or moods. They can be positive, like happiness, joy, or excitement. They can also be negative, like sadness, anger, or worry.

Actions: These are things we do. They can be things like riding a bike, petting a dog, or taking a test.

What's important to know is that these three things are connected. How we think can make us feel a certain way, which can make us act a certain way.

For example, let's say you have a big soccer game tomorrow. You might be feeling a little nervous. But what if you thought to yourself, "Tomorrow I'm going to try my best. Whether my team wins or loses, I always have fun at my games." How might you feel? Thinking this way might help you feel a little less nervous. Maybe you would even tell your friends about the game and ask them to come.

Now, what would happen if you thought to yourself, "Tomorrow is going to be terrible! My team always loses, and I definitely won't have any fun." How would you feel? Thinking this way would probably make you feel even more nervous—and you sure wouldn't be looking forward to your game. Maybe you'd put your soccer sweater in a drawer so you wouldn't have to be reminded about soccer.

The same steps happen with OCD. You might think you'll get very sick if you don't wash your hands a certain number of times. That's a thought. Then the thought of getting very sick makes you feel worried. That's a feeling. This makes you wash your hands again and again. That's an action.

As you and your family go through this workbook and learn different tools for dealing with OCD, try to always remember that your thoughts, feelings, and actions are connected. You'll slowly learn to face your fears, and you'll prove to yourself that your OCD thoughts are wrong and that nothing bad happens when you don't give in to your compulsions. You'll learn to take the power away from OCD. *You will be the powerful one—not OCD.*

OCD CAN'T STOP ME!

Having OCD can make you feel scared or worried. But you're not alone. Did you know that there are over half a million other kids in the United States who are struggling with OCD?

Sometimes when you're going through a hard time, it helps to say kind or encouraging things to yourself. These words will help you get through it. What are some things you can say to yourself to stay positive? How can you be your own cheer-leader? To get you started, here are a few things you can say:

- "Having OCD is hard. Standing up to OCD feels even harder. But I know I can do this!"

- "OCD takes up so much of my time. The more I practice using my tools, the better I'll feel. I'll have so much more free time to have fun."

- "I'm a normal kid. I'm not weird. My OCD doesn't get to say who I am."

- "When I get stuck, I need to remember it's my OCD talking."

- "Things might seem scary now, but there are lots of kids going through what I'm going through. I'm not alone."

- "I'm brave. OCD is a bully. I can—and I will—stand up to it!"

- "I'm tougher than OCD!"

- "Sometimes it seems that OCD has all the power. But I have to remember that I'm the powerful one. I'm stronger than my OCD."

LET'S GO TO A PARTY!

Look at the picture on page 35. Gino is having his eighth birthday party. Do you see all the fun things going on? All of his friends are there, and there's a cake and lots of presents; it's a fun party!

What actions do you see? Remember, actions are things that we do. Most of the time, we can see them being done. Starting at the top of the page, draw a line through the party, but make sure to visit Gino and his friends along the way!

When you get to each kid, write a few words next to them that might describe what they are thinking and how they are feeling. It looks like Gino is about to open a gift! What do you think he is thinking about right now? Uh-oh, Gino's friend Sarah dropped her cake. I wonder how she feels about that.

Try to notice how actions, thoughts, and feelings are connected. Have fun visiting the party!

BE STILL

Sit still for a few moments. Take in your surroundings. Now, close your eyes. Notice all the thoughts that pop into your head, no matter how small or strange. What are some of the thoughts you have?

In the space below, draw a few of the thoughts, words, or pictures that pop into your head. Are some of them happy? Are some of them sad? Are some of them really weird? How do they make you feel?

Try doing this activity with someone else, then compare pictures. Do you have some of the same thoughts?

You Can Do This!

In this chapter, you've learned a lot about OCD. You learned what obsessions and compulsions are. You learned how they're related and how the OCD loop works. You learned that OCD has a lot to do with the brain and how your brain can get "stuck." You learned the difference between everyday worry and OCD. You learned how a little bit of worry can actually be a good thing. And finally, you learned how thoughts, feelings, and actions are related. That's a lot of learning. Great job!

In the next chapter, you're going to learn how to be an OCD detective. To change something, we have to know what it is first. Then we can deal with it. Are you ready to start learning how to spot OCD? Put your detective hat on and let's get started!

CHAPTER 2

HOW TO BE AN OCD DETECTIVE

Now that you know a little more about what OCD is, you might be thinking, "How do I face something so difficult?" Sometimes OCD makes you feel like you have to check things over and over or wash your hands again and again. Maybe you have a lot of worries that start with the words, "What if?" Or maybe you often ask your parents or teachers, "Are you sure?" With OCD, you often feel "stuck."

But there's no need to fear. You're going to become an expert in OCD and learn how to get unstuck. Just like a detective, you're going to learn to notice things. You'll learn the different ways OCD can pop up and get in your way, stopping you from having fun and living a happy life. Most importantly, you'll learn to stand up to OCD. Are you ready, detective?

What Are Obsessions?

We all have an imagination. Our brains can come up with some really creative and interesting thoughts. You can think of a fairy tale with giant castles and magical creatures. Or you can think of the fun things you want to do during the summer. Thousands of thoughts come into your head every single day.

Some thoughts are exciting, like thinking about a fun vacation or a friend's birthday party. Some thoughts make you worried, like thinking about getting into trouble or taking a big test. And some thoughts can be silly, exciting, boring, and everything in between. So many thoughts!

For kids without OCD, thoughts come and go with no problem. With OCD, your brain can get "stuck" on certain thoughts or images. They don't go through the sifter.

Sometimes, your brain has trouble telling the difference between the thoughts in your mind and the real world. OCD might make you have thoughts that are scary or don't make sense.

These thoughts keep coming back and won't stop bothering you. You don't want them there, but they just keep replaying in your mind on an endless loop. They seem to come out of nowhere. You try not to think about them and push them away, but it's so hard to do. They just won't leave you alone!

These types of thoughts are called *obsessions*.

Let's look at a story about Jacob, who is struggling with obsessions.

JACOB'S STORY

Jacob is 11 years old and has OCD. He's getting ready to go play a baseball game. He remembers his team is playing their rival today, the Falcons.

At the game, Jacob sees his teammate and best friend, Fidel, who gives him a high five. Jacob suddenly worries to himself, "What if my hands weren't clean? What if I gave Fidel my germs? What if he gets sick and something terrible happens to him?" Jacob can't seem to stop thinking about something bad happening to his best friend. He asks Fidel, "Are you okay?" again and again.

Jacob tries to calm down, but he can't get rid of the scary thoughts and images of his friend being "contaminated" and getting sick. He just can't get the image out of his head of something bad happening.

FEELING LIKE JACOB

Do you ever feel like Jacob did? With OCD, scary or uncomfortable thoughts that you don't want just pop into your head. Some kids might be worried about germs or getting sick. Other kids might have worries or doubts about not doing things right. OCD can even make kids think of upsetting images of them hurting their best friend, even though they'd never, ever want to do that.

It's important to practice learning the difference between every-day thoughts and obsessions. Remember, everyday thoughts are ones you don't usually get "stuck" on. They also usually make sense. For example, Jacob remembers he's playing the Falcons today. That's an everyday thought.

Obsessions are ones you get "stuck" on. And you don't want them there. For Jacob, one of his obsessions is his best friend, Fidel, getting "contaminated"—which is another way of saying getting dirty or sick.

Here are some other examples to help you understand the difference between everyday thoughts and obsessions.

EVERYDAY THOUGHT	OBSESSION
"I wonder what's for dinner tonight?"	"Dinner is going to be undercooked and I'll get sick."
"I definitely locked the door; I remember locking it."	"Even though I locked the door twice already, what if it's not locked? I need to go back and make sure."
"I need to be careful when using scissors."	"What if I accidentally hurt someone while using scissors?"
"I should read this chapter for homework carefully."	"I need to read this chapter for homework perfectly or else something bad will happen."
"I finished my homework"	"It looks like I finished my homework, but I need to ask my mom again and again to make sure I did."
"My favorite stuffed animal is my penguin named Freezer."	"My stuffed animals need to be in a certain order."
"I felt a bump when I was riding my bike this morning. It was probably just a rock."	"I felt a bump when I rode my bike this morning. What if I ran over an animal? I should go back and double-check to make sure."
"I pet my dog. I should probably wash my hands."	"I can't pet my dog because he has germs and I'll get really sick."

WRITING DOWN YOUR THOUGHTS

Now you try. Write down some everyday thoughts that you have. Remember, an everyday thought is usually something that's not very scary and doesn't get "stuck" in your head. You're normally okay with it being there and don't feel the need to push it away. Everyday thoughts can be happy, sad, boring, or silly.

Then, write down some of your obsessions. Remember, an obsession is usually something that makes you feel really anxious and that you get "stuck" on. Obsessions are usually scary or uncomfortable. You definitely don't want them, and you might even try to push them away.

EVERYDAY THOUGHT	OBSESSION

You Are in Charge

To change something, we have to understand the problem in a very detailed way. We can't change what we don't know about. That's why it's really important to be an OCD detective and to learn as much as you can about your OCD. You need to become an expert!

Everyone's OCD is a little different. Some kids have worries about germs and things not being clean. Other kids have thoughts and images about getting hurt or hurting others—even though they'd never want to do that. OCD makes some kids doubt themselves and makes them unsure if they did or didn't do something. In other words, no two kids have exactly the same OCD.

Let's practice getting to know your OCD better. Remember that OCD has two parts: The first is thoughts you don't want to have that won't stop bothering you. These thoughts cause you to feel bad or worried and are called obsessions. The second part is what you do to make yourself feel better. When you feel bad, you want the bad feeling to go away, so you do something to make the feeling get better or stop. The problem is that the feeling only goes away for a little while and then comes back, so you have to do the thing again and again. These are called compulsions.

Let's focus on the first part, obsessions, so you can learn more about them.

WHAT ARE YOUR OBSESSIONS?

Below is a list of obsessions. Remember, an obsession is a thought or image that pops into your head and keeps bothering you no matter how hard you try to make it stop.

Read each item carefully and put a check mark (✓) next to the ones that are true for you. There are no right or wrong answers. If you have other obsessions that aren't on this list, write them down on the blank lines.

- ❑ I can't stop thinking about bad things.
- ❑ After I do something, I'm not sure I really did it.
- ❑ I worry that something bad is going to happen to someone I care about.
- ❑ When I throw things away, I worry I might need them again.
- ❑ I think I made a mistake, even when I did something very carefully.
- ❑ I have bad thoughts about losing control and hurting someone.
- ❑ I worry about hurting someone's feelings when I don't mean to.
- ❑ I have bad thoughts about losing control and hurting myself.
- ❑ I worry that my homework isn't done right, even after I check it.
- ❑ I worry that my food is full of germs.
- ❑ Even when I study really hard, I'm sure I'll fail my test.
- ❑ I worry that I'm secretly a bad person who does bad things.
- ❑ I worry that I'm really sick.
- ❑ _____
- ❑ _____
- ❑ _____

Let's now focus on the second part, compulsions, so you can learn more about them.

What Are Compulsions?

We all have things we do almost the same way every day. We brush our teeth. We eat dinner. We turn off our bedroom light at night. With OCD, these everyday things can be very difficult. Sometimes with OCD, you feel like you need to do things that just don't make sense.

These types of actions are called *compulsions*.

Let's look at a story about Nancy, who is nine years old and struggling with compulsions.

NANCY'S STORY

Nancy eats breakfast at 7:00 a.m. with her parents and her brother. They're having eggs—her favorite! But before sitting down, she walks around the table exactly three times. If she doesn't, she worries something bad will happen. For Nancy, things just don't feel right unless she circles the table before eating.

Nancy takes a big bite of food, then asks her parents, "Are you sure the eggs are cooked?" They say, "Of course." But Nancy is still not convinced. She asks them a few more times. "But what if they're not?" she says. "What if I get sick?"

She then turns to her brother and asks him to wash his hands again. Nancy worries that he may have touched her fork. What if he got his germs on it?

She then goes to the refrigerator to check the expiration date on the carton of eggs—just to be sure. If the eggs are even one day past the expiration date, Nancy worries that the food has gone bad and is dangerous to eat.

FEELING LIKE NANCY

Do you ever feel like Nancy? With OCD, sometimes you feel you have to do something a certain way, or count things a specific number of times, or do something until it feels "just right." Remember, these actions are called compulsions.

Some kids might check over and over again that their bedroom door is closed. Other kids might say something out loud a certain number of times. OCD might also make kids ask questions even when they already know the answers. Other compulsions include doing things evenly, saying certain words, or touching things a specific way.

Let's practice learning the difference between habits and compulsions. Habits are things that you do every day that don't usually feel scary or stressful. For example, Nancy eats breakfast at 7:00 a.m. every day with her family. That's a habit.

Compulsions are things that OCD tells you that you have to do, maybe a certain way, or a certain number of times—or until things feel "just right." One of Nancy's compulsions is to circle the table three times before she can sit down to eat.

Here are some other examples to help you understand the difference between habits and compulsions.

HABIT	COMPULSION
Washing your hands for 10 seconds, thinking, "They're clean now."	Washing your hands for 10 minutes, thinking the whole time, "What if they're not clean yet?"
Asking your teacher if you have homework due.	Asking your teacher over and over if she is sure you don't have homework due tomorrow.
Locking your front door at night.	Locking and unlocking your front door 20 times.
Walking up the stairs to bed.	Counting your steps as you go up the stairs and starting over if you did it "wrong."
Saying bedtime prayers.	Needing to say bedtime prayers in a certain order and feeling guilty if you don't.
Kissing your parent goodnight.	Kissing your parent on one cheek and getting very upset if you can't kiss them on the other cheek.
Getting dressed in the morning.	Needing to put on certain clothes and take them off again until it feels "just right."

HABITS VS. COMPULSIONS

Write some everyday habits that you have. Remember, a habit is something you usually do every day that's not very scary and you don't get "stuck" on.

Now, write down some of your compulsions. Remember, a compulsion is something you do or say to make your worries or bad feelings go away.

Remember, everyone's OCD is different. Just like you learned about the thoughts you have that won't leave you alone, now you'll learn about the things you have to do or say to make the thoughts go away or feel better. Some kids have to wash themselves again and again. Other kids have to repeat words or numbers over and over. OCD makes other kids tap or touch things a certain way.

HABIT	COMPULSION

WHAT ARE YOUR COMPULSIONS?

Below is a list of compulsions. Remember, a compulsion is something you do or say a certain way, or number of times, or until things feel "just right." You do this to push away bad or scary thoughts and feel less worried.

Read each item carefully and put a check mark (✓) next to the ones that are true for you. There are no right or wrong answers. If there are other things that you have to do or say over and over that aren't on this list, write them down on the blank lines.

- ❑ I keep things I don't need anymore.
- ❑ I feel like I need to wash my hands a lot.
- ❑ I use sanitizer a lot when my hands feel dirty.
- ❑ I check my homework again and again.
- ❑ I ask people questions that I know the answer to.
- ❑ I need to count certain things.
- ❑ I repeat certain words over and over again.
- ❑ I arrange things in a certain way.
- ❑ I tap things a certain number of times.
- ❑ I do things over and over again until they feel "just right."
- ❑ I repeat the same question again and again.
- ❑ I keep my toys even when they're broken.
- ❑ When I have a bad thought, I have to repeat a certain word.
- ❑ My schoolbag has to be packed the same way every day.
- ❑ When I put something away, I check again and again to be sure it's there.
- ❑ I check locks and windows even when I know they are locked.
- ❑ I say prayers a lot more than most kids.
- ❑ I tell my parents when I have done something wrong, even when it is very small.
- ❑ I have to walk in a certain way that is difficult.
- ❑ _____
- ❑ _____
- ❑ _____

Let's Take Action

Now that you know more about your OCD, you can start to take action. There are many ways you can stand up to your OCD. In the next sections, you're going to learn about three tools you can use.

The first tool is called the "Thought Changer." Unfortunately, we can't just change how we feel by choosing to feel something else. What we can do is change how we think. Sometimes when we get really nervous or angry, it's because we're thinking in ways that are not balanced and not helpful. The "Thought Changer" tool will teach you healthier, more balanced ways of thinking.

The second tool is called the "Observer." With this tool, you watch (or *observe*) your scary or upsetting thoughts. Instead of trying to push them away, you just notice them. You don't say they shouldn't be there. You just observe them. By doing this, you take the power away from your OCD thoughts.

The third tool is called "Test It Out." With OCD, you often feel that you can only push your scary thoughts away by counting or repeating things over and over. With "Test It Out," you find out if that's really true. Instead of doing or saying the things you normally do to make those thoughts go away, you try to stop yourself. By slowly facing your fears, you prove to yourself that your OCD thoughts are wrong.

As you learn to use the tools, keep in mind that how you think, how you feel, and how you act are connected. Also remember that obsessions are usually thoughts and compulsions are usually actions. Both of these have a really big effect on your feelings.

Are you ready to learn how to use these tools to stand up to your OCD? Let's get started.

TOOL #1: THE "THOUGHT CHANGER"

We can't change how we feel just because we want to. For example, if we're feeling anxious, we can't just replace feeling anxious with feeling happy. Wouldn't it be nice if we could?

The good news is that we can change how we think.

With the "Thought Changer" tool, you change your thoughts to help change your feelings by thinking in a healthier, more balanced way. If you're feeling anxious about something, go back and check how you're thinking. Are you thinking things through? What are the facts? What is the evidence? What is the chance that the thing you're worried about will actually happen? And even if it did happen, how bad would that really be?

Here's a simple way to remember the "Thought Changer" tool: "I'm not my thoughts. And thoughts can be changed."

Let's look at a story about Emilio, who uses the "Thought Changer" tool.

EMILIO'S STORY

Emilio is nine years old and has OCD. As he gets ready to go to sleep, his little puppy Spotty jumps up to join him in bed. Emilio is worried if he pets Spotty, he'll get his dog's germs and get sick. Spotty starts licking Emilio and right away Emilio starts feeling anxious. He starts to have scary thoughts like, "What if I accidentally touched some of Spotty's slobber? Ew! And what if it got in my mouth? What if I get sick? That would be terrible!"

Emilio takes a few deep breaths and thinks, "I've slept with my dog every night for months now, and not once have I gotten sick. And what if some slobber did get on me? So what? It's a little bit gross but not all that bad. And the chance of me getting sick from my dog is almost impossible. But even if I did get sick, even that wouldn't be the worst thing in the world. I've been sick before, and yeah, it's not fun, but I get through it every time."

By calming himself down and thinking clearly, Emilio is able to stop his scary thoughts about getting sick.

FEELING LIKE EMILIO

Have there ever been times when you felt like Emilio? Even though Emilio's OCD makes him worry about getting sick, he's able to challenge his thoughts. He thinks hard about what he fears—getting dog slobber on him and getting sick. He knows that's not really the worst thing in the world. Emilio is able to find a balanced thought, which makes him feel less anxious.

With the "Thought Changer" tool, you look at the evidence and the facts—like a detective would—and change your thoughts to go with the evidence.

LET'S USE THE "THOUGHT CHANGER" TOOL

Think of some thoughts you sometimes have that you don't like and that keep coming back. Write them down on the lines below. Now write down how those thoughts make you feel.

After writing down your thoughts and feelings, try to challenge your thoughts by asking yourself the questions below.

- Can I be 100 percent sure that this will happen?
- Can I really see into the future? Am I a fortune teller? Do I have a special crystal ball?
- Are there other ways to look at this?
- What's the worst that could happen? How bad would that be? Could I get through it?

Do you notice any difference in how you feel after? When you think in a more balanced way, you often feel better!

TOOL #2: THE "OBSERVER"

Let's play a game: For the next 30 seconds, do not think of a hippopotamus in a bathing suit. Whatever you do, try not to think about a hippopotamus in a bathing suit. You can think of anything else in the world, but not a hippopotamus in a bathing suit.

Ready? Go!

How long could you last? One second? Maybe three seconds? What we can learn from the hippopotamus-in-a-bathing-suit game is this: Telling ourselves not to think about something only makes it worse.

Another tool you can use to stand up to OCD is called the "Observer" tool. With this tool, you notice your thoughts without judging them. It's just like when we watch clouds in the sky. The clouds come. We look at them. The clouds slowly move away, and then they're gone. We don't judge the clouds or say that they should or shouldn't be there. We just observe them.

A helpful way to notice and observe your OCD thoughts is by adding the words, "I'm having a thought that . . ." or, "My OCD is telling me that . . ." before your OCD thought.

For example, maybe your OCD is making you think, "I'm going to get sick if I don't wash my hands just right." That thought would probably make you feel pretty anxious. But you could say, "I'm having a thought that I'm going to get sick if I don't wash my hands just right." Or you could say, "My OCD is telling me that I'm going to get sick if I don't wash my hands just right."

Describing your thoughts in these different ways can help you feel less anxious. When you add those extra words, you remind yourself it's just an OCD thought, not reality.

Here's a simple way to remember the "Observer" tool: Thoughts are just thoughts. They're not facts. They're just ideas.

Let's look at a story about Ling, who uses the "Observer" tool.

LING'S STORY

Ling is seven years old and has OCD. It's a relaxing Sunday afternoon. She's playing a board game with her sister, Hanh, whom she loves very much. Sometimes Ling's OCD makes her have scary thoughts that seem to come out of nowhere. When she has these thoughts, Ling often feels she needs to say exactly what she's thinking and tell another person her thoughts. If not, she feels guilty and uncomfortable and anxious.

All of a sudden, Ling feels frightened. She has a scary thought that her sister will get hurt on her walk to school tomorrow. Ling can't seem to push the thought away. She has an urge, which is a strong feeling, to tell her sister what she's thinking.

But instead of giving in to her OCD, she thinks to herself: "I'm having a thought that my sister will get hurt. This is my OCD talking. Just because I think about my sister getting hurt, it doesn't mean that she will. It's just a thought. I have thoughts all day long. This is just another one. I can handle this!"

Ling focuses on the board game. When the OCD thought comes creeping back in, she notices it. She doesn't push it away. She doesn't say, "I would never want my sister to get hurt." She just observes the thought. She even says, "Hello thought." Once again, Ling focuses her attention back on the board game and the thought becomes less and less scary. "It's just a thought," she repeats to herself.

FEELING LIKE LING

Have there ever been times when you felt like Ling? Even though Ling's OCD makes her feel she needs to tell her sister what she's thinking, she decides to just wait and observe. She tells herself that even though the thought of something bad happening to her sister is really scary, it's just a thought. And thoughts are just thoughts; they don't have the power to hurt us.

With the "Observer" tool, you don't judge your thoughts. You just observe them.

LET'S USE THE "OBSERVER" TOOL

Think of some thoughts you have sometimes that you can't push away.
Write them on the lines below, after the words, "I'm having a thought
that . . ." Then reread each sentence. Do the thoughts feel different when
you're reminded that they're just thoughts?

   Try reading the sentences one more time. The more you remind yourself that your OCD thoughts are ideas and not facts, the less power they
will have.

"I'm having a thought that _____

_____."

"I'm having a thought that _____

_____."

"I'm having a thought that _____

_____."

"I'm having a thought that _____

_____."

"I'm having a thought that _____

_____."

TOOL #3: "TEST IT OUT"

One more tool you can use to stand up to OCD is called "Test It Out." While the other two tools focus on your thoughts, this tool focuses on your actions.

OCD tells you that the only way to make your worries go away is to count, check, or repeat things again and again. But do you ever wonder if that's really true? With the "Test It Out" tool, you do an OCD experiment to find out.

First, think of the things that OCD tells you are scary. Now, try your very best to stop doing the things you normally do to make those thoughts go away. In other words, try not to do the repeated actions, like counting or tapping. What happens when you don't do these actions? Did the scary thoughts come true? Or did nothing happen?

With "Test It Out," you slowly face your fears and learn that your OCD thoughts are wrong. The OCD experiment proves that nothing bad happens when you don't give in to your compulsions.

Here's a simple way to remember the "Test It Out" tool: Testing proves that OCD thoughts are wrong. Nothing bad happens when I don't give in to them.

Let's look to a story about Ashley, who uses the "Test It Out" tool.

ASHLEY'S STORY

Ashley is 10 years old and has OCD. It's time to do her homework. Her OCD tells her that she needs to write her name a certain way. If she doesn't, her OCD makes her feel she needs to erase and rewrite her name again and again until it feels right. Sometimes, it takes her 15 minutes just to get started—how frustrating!

This time, she decides to do something different. Ashley wants to see what will happen if she doesn't rewrite. In fact, she challenges herself to write her name wrong—on purpose. She takes a blank sheet of paper and tries writing her name many different ways. First, she writes her name crooked. She starts to feel nervous. She feels in her right hand the urge to take her eraser and erase her name. She puts down her pencil and sits with that nervous feeling.

At first, it's really hard! Ashley wants so badly to take her pencil and make it "just right." She continues to look at her name and focus on just how crooked it is. After a little time goes by, she notices her worry has gone down.

Feeling brave, she thinks, "Hmm, I wonder what will happen now if I spell my name even more wrong." Ashley takes her pencil and writes her name like this: "aShLeY." At first, she feels very, very uncomfortable. But soon, the urge to rewrite her name starts to get a little weaker. And her anxiety begins to go away a little bit.

FEELING LIKE ASHLEY

Have there ever been times when you felt like Ashley? Even though her OCD makes her feel like she needs to write and rewrite her name just right, she does exactly the opposite—on purpose. What's really interesting is that even though it's very hard at first for her to resist, which means to try and stop, the urge to erase and rewrite her name eventually gets weaker.

With the "Test It Out" tool, you don't give in to OCD. You stand up to it.

LET'S USE THE "TEST IT OUT" TOOL

Think of some things that OCD tells you are scary or difficult. On the lines below, list at least five things. Now, on a scale of 1–10, decide how scary or difficult each of those things is. One means that it's not scary or difficult at all. Ten means it's extremely scary or difficult. Five is somewhere in the middle.

Try to think of some things that are not scary/easy (1–3), sort of scary/medium (4–7), and very scary/hard (8–10). You aren't going to use the "Test It Out" tool just yet, but it'll be good to get a head start thinking more about your OCD. Here are some examples of how your "Test It Out" list might look:

- Touching the refrigerator door and not washing my hands right away: 6

- Purposely mixing up the order of my stuffed animals: 3

- Locking the door only one time and walking away: 8

IT'S OKAY TO TALK ABOUT OCD

Telling friends, family, and teachers about your OCD is okay to do! Whether you want to tell others is up to you. Either way, there's no need to feel embarrassed or bad about yourself. Remember, there is nothing wrong with you for having OCD.

Let's say you're doing a math assignment in class. You know that 3 × 9 is 27. But your OCD is telling you that it might be the wrong answer, and the number 27 just isn't written the way you want it to be. So, you write, cross out, and rewrite your answer over and over. If another classmate or teacher asks what you're doing, you could try saying something like this:

"I have OCD, which makes me get stuck on things. It makes thoughts pop into my head that I just can't stop thinking about and makes me feel terrible. To make these thoughts and feelings go away, I have to do things a certain way or number of times. Or sometimes I have to count, check, or repeat things until it feels just right. It's really frustrating, but I'm working really hard on it."

Sometimes, kids and adults think that OCD means just wanting things to be clean or organized. It can feel really frustrating when others say, "I'm such a neat freak, too! I'm *so OCD*." If someone says this, you could use this chance to teach them about OCD. Maybe you could say something like this:

"OCD isn't about just liking things to be clean. Kids can have OCD and also be messy. OCD makes me feel stuck. It makes me feel locked into things and repeat things over and over. I try to stop, but it's really, really hard to."

You're Doing Great!

Amazing job! In this chapter, you learned how to be an OCD detective. You learned what makes your OCD unique. You learned how to spot the specific thoughts that won't leave you alone and tell the difference between everyday thoughts and obsessions. You also learned how to spot the specific actions you have to do or say over and over and tell the difference between everyday habits and compulsions. You had a review on how thoughts, feelings, and actions are connected. Finally, you learned about three tools you can use to help you stand up to your OCD.

In the next chapter, you'll practice using your three new tools: "The Thought Changer," "The Observer," and "Test It Out." You're doing great! Let's keep going!

CHAPTER 3

STANDING UP TO OCD

By now, you're becoming a real OCD expert! You've learned so much about your thoughts, feelings, and actions. In the last chapter, you started learning about a few tools that can help you stand up to OCD. In this chapter, you're going to put them to the test.

Remember, these tools will take a lot of practice. Just like taking one tennis lesson won't make you an amazing tennis player, practicing with the tools one or two times won't make your OCD 100 percent better. But you can do this! Your hard work will pay off.

Some of the activities in this chapter might seem really scary or hard at first. But the more you practice, the easier they'll get. It'll help to work with a parent or caregiver for extra support. You're going to show your OCD who's the boss. And you will start to see progress. Eventually, you'll look back at things you once thought were difficult, and they'll be easier. It might seem like OCD has all the power right now. But remember, you are the powerful one. And you're brave for facing your OCD. You've got this!

Let's Build a Ladder

When things are hard, sometimes it's best to start with the easiest things first and work your way up.

For example, let's say you want to learn to play the piano. Before learning to play a really difficult song, you have to learn the basics. First, you have to know what all those black and white keys mean. Eighty-eight keys—wow, so many!

Then, you might start practicing scales. *Do, Re, Mi, Fa, Sol, La, Ti, Do*. Next, you learn to play several keys at once. *Do-Mi-Sol*. Maybe you then learn to play using both hands. Before you know it, you're playing a real song. Way to go!

Once you're a really good piano player, what happens when you look back at all the basic things you learned at the very beginning, like naming the notes and playing the scales? They seem so much easier, even though when you first started, they seemed almost impossible. Things you once thought that you would never be able to do are simple now!

The same is true with your OCD. Just like you would start slowly on the piano, you'll start slowly when you face your OCD. You're going to take this at your own pace.

So, first things first. You're going to list all the scary and frustrating things OCD makes you do. To help you out, let's look at a story about Maria.

MARIA'S STORY

Maria is 11 years old and has OCD. A lot of her thoughts have to do with being clean. She doesn't give her parents hugs because they're "germy." She doesn't sit on the couch where her dog sits because he's "germy," too! She also doesn't touch doorknobs, drawers, elevator buttons, or the car door handle. Anything that other people touch, Maria won't touch. She doesn't walk barefoot in the house, since her feet would step on lots of dirt and dust and things that might make her sick.

Maria carries hand sanitizer at all times—"just in case." She takes really long showers and uses lots and lots of soap. But she has to soap first, then shampoo, and it has to be in that order. Maria also dries herself off with many towels. This also has to be done in a certain order until it feels "just right." If a towel accidentally touches the bathroom floor, she needs to find a new one and start all over.

MARIA'S LADDER

Do you ever have times when you feel like Maria? Her OCD tells her that almost everything she touches has germs. In Maria's mind, if she touches germs, that would be terrible. So, to avoid getting germs on her, Maria has many things she does to "protect" her. How difficult it must be for Maria!

For Maria to stand up to her OCD, the first step is for her to write down all of the scary things OCD tells her she needs to avoid so she doesn't get "germy."

Maria's list looks like this:

- Walk in the living room barefoot for three minutes

- Dry off with only one towel

- Only brush my hair for 30 seconds

- Walk in the living room barefoot for 10 minutes after having friends over

- Touch one elevator button at my doctor's office with one finger

- Pet my dog using only my left hand

- Dry off with a towel that touched the bathroom floor

- Let my dog lick my right hand

- Open the car door with my right hand, then give my mom a hug

- Take a shower for only 10 minutes

Doing these things would be difficult for Maria! Some of these things might be easier than others. Some might be harder than others. So, the next step for Maria is to build her OCD ladder.

Maria does this by looking through her list and thinking about how hard it would be to face the fears that OCD tells her are scary. At the very bottom of the ladder—the first rung—she puts things that would be pretty easy and not that bad. At the very top of the ladder—the last rung—she puts things that would be really, really, really hard and scary. In the middle of the ladder she puts things that would be not too easy, but not too hard, either.

1. Let my dog lick my right hand

2. Open the car door with my right hand, then give my mom a hug

3. Dry off with a towel that touched the bathroom floor

4. Dry off with only one towel

5. Take a shower for only 10 minutes

6. Walk in the living room barefoot for 10 minutes after having friends over

7. Walk in the living room barefoot for three minutes

8. Only brush hair for 30 seconds

9. Touch one elevator button at my doctor's office with one finger

10. Pet my dog using only my left hand

Do you see that Maria was able to make some of her worries a little less scary by mixing them up? For example, Maria's OCD tells her that petting the dog with her left hand is harder than petting the dog with her right hand. Showering for 10 minutes is still hard, but not as hard as for only five minutes.

Not every ladder rung has to have something next to it. If you can only think of five things to put on your ladder right now, that's okay. You can always add more to it later.

TIME TO BUILD YOUR LADDER

Think of all the things that OCD tells you are scary. These can be thoughts that pop into your head and don't leave you alone. These can also be things you try to avoid because of your OCD, like going certain places or doing things the "wrong" way.

Now, think about how hard or scary each of these things would be if you weren't allowed to do your compulsions. Write things that would be super hard at the very top. A little further down, write things that would still be difficult but not as bad as the things at the top of the ladder.

Keep going until you reach the bottom rung. Remember, as you go down the ladder, things should get a little easier. And it's okay if not every rung on the ladder has something on it. Just try your best to think of easy, medium, and hard things. When you're done, number the items.

Now, start building!

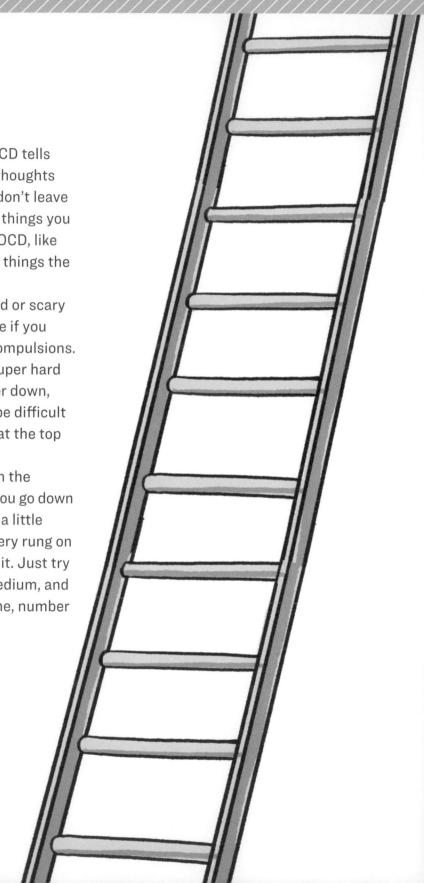

IT'S OKAY TO FEEL A LITTLE UNCOMFORTABLE

Standing up to your OCD can be really hard. Sometimes, saying "no" to your OCD and facing the things OCD says you can't face is very challenging. But if anyone can do it, it's you. Here are a few tips and tricks to help you stay focused and work hard.

Keep track of your progress: In the last activity, you gave numbers to things OCD tells you are scary. Hold on to these! As you keep resisting your OCD, write down these numbers every week. Things that were a 9 on a difficulty scale of 1–10 the first week might drop to a 5 on the scale the second week. This means that things that used to be at the top of the ladder dropped down a little. And this means they're not as scary as they were before— and you're making progress. Fantastic!

Lean on your friends or family for support: What you're doing is really hard stuff. When the going gets tough, be sure to reach out to a close friend, sibling, parent, or teacher for some encouragement.

Give yourself some credit: To a kid without OCD, some of the things you're doing might not seem like a big deal. But for you, stopping yourself from doing the things OCD tells you to do is super difficult. So, you deserve some credit. Give yourself a pat on the back!

Think ahead: All those scary thoughts and all that checking, counting, washing, and repeating takes up a lot of your time. Think ahead to all the free time you'll have as you stand up to your OCD. What fun things will you do with all that extra time?

Reward yourself: You've been working really hard. Ask your parent or caregiver if it's time for a reward.

STAYING MOTIVATED

Think of some tricks that you can use to stay motivated. On some of the lines below, write down the names of some people you could lean on for support. This could be a friend, a sibling, a teacher—anyone you feel you can trust who would be positive and supportive.

On the other lines, write down some things you're very excited about and looking forward to doing for fun as you start to see progress standing up to your OCD.

Let's Start Climbing

Amazing job so far! You've done great work being an OCD detective. Now that you've written down all the difficult things on your ladder, it's time to start climbing. Remember the three tools you learned in the last chapter? They were "The Thought Changer," "The Observer," and "Test It Out."

Let's look at a story about Charlie, who has built his OCD ladder and is starting to use the first tool, "The Thought Changer." For Charlie, thoughts about doing well and checking things in his bedroom are toward the bottom of his ladder, so that's where he decides to start.

CHARLIE'S STORY

Charlie is eight years old and has OCD. His OCD makes him have unwanted thoughts about something bad happening if he doesn't do things a certain way.

Every night, Charlie has a routine. A routine is a set of activities that someone does in the same way everyday. But this isn't a regular routine, like brushing his teeth and getting ready for bed; this is an OCD routine. It's really, really hard for Charlie, and he feels he needs to do things in a very specific order. If not, bad things will happen. Like tomorrow: Charlie has a statewide spelling bee that he's been practicing really hard for. He worries if he doesn't do his nighttime routine just right, he'll get last place and his parents will be really disappointed in him.

One of Charlie's routines is to check under the bed three times. Then, he has to make sure the last number of his clock ends on an even number. If it doesn't, he needs to continue checking under the bed over and over until the clock ends on a 2, 4, 6, or 8.

Charlie also has to pull his covers back in a certain way. First, he pulls down the comforter. Then, he stacks and unstacks his pillows. Next, he makes sure the corners of his sheets are completely tucked in. Finally, he can hop into bed.

But this time, Charlie thinks, "I'm going to try my best tomorrow at the spelling bee. Whether I check three times or three hundred times has nothing to do with how I'll do tomorrow. What matters is how much

I prepared, and I studied super hard for this the past month. So, chances are I'll do just fine. And even if I do get last place, so what? I still made it this far, which is something to be proud of."

FEELING LIKE CHARLIE

Do you ever have times when you feel like Charlie? He has thoughts pop into his head that something bad will happen. This time, he's worried he's going to do horribly at his spelling bee. To make this thought go away, he gets "stuck" checking under his bed over and over again. How frustrating!

But Charlie is able to stop his OCD loop by changing how he thinks about things. He challenges his OCD thoughts head on. He reminds himself that what really affects how well he'll do at his spelling bee is how much he studies, not how many times he checks under his bed.

Charlie also catches himself thinking about the worst thing that could happen. He remembers that he studied hard, so the chance of him getting last place are pretty low. And he even goes one step further. Charlie reminds himself that even if he does come in last place, he should still be proud of himself for getting as far as he did. After all, he made it to the state championship, which is pretty good proof that Charlie knows a thing or two about spelling.

Keep Climbing

Sometimes, OCD makes you doubt whether you did or didn't do something. For some kids, this might be worrying if their backpack was zipped "just right" after they put their homework in it. For others, it might be asking questions about things they already know the answer to. OCD also makes some kids worry that they might hurt someone, even though they know they would never want to do that.

Let's look at a story about Feng, who uses the "Observer" tool.

FENG'S STORY

Feng is 10 years old and has OCD. Sometimes Feng's OCD makes him worry deep down about things he knows he didn't do. Still, when these thoughts or pictures pop into his head, he can't seem to get rid of them. He needs to go back and "make sure" or ask other people questions over and over.

For example, Feng just finished a vocabulary quiz in English class. The teacher collected everyone's exams. Now it's lunchtime—yay! But while sitting with his friends enjoying his PB&J sandwich, a thought pops into Feng's head: "Did I cheat on that exam?" Feng, of course, has never, ever cheated. But that pesky thought just won't go away. His OCD won't leave him alone.

In the past, when Feng would have these doubts, he'd run back to class and find his teacher and say, "Mrs. Appleton, I think I cheated on the test. Did you see me cheat? Are you sure I didn't?" He'd also ask his friends, "Hey guys, did you notice me looking at your answers? Did I cheat on that test?"

But this time, Feng is able to recognize that this is his OCD talking. He remembers that, in the past, even though he'd feel better when his friends and teachers calmed him down by saying that he didn't cheat, the feeling only lasted a few minutes. More and more doubts would race through his head. It was an endless loop of doubting and asking.

So, this time, Feng tells himself that this is just a thought. "I know that this is you trying to trick me, OCD. I'm not going to ask my teachers and friends if I cheated. I'm not going to say I did cheat. I'm not going to say I didn't cheat. I'm just going to see you for what you are: a thought."

Just like a leaf in a stream, Feng's OCD thought floats away. Feng watches it leave, then brings his attention back to his buddies and that delicious PB&J sandwich.

FEELING LIKE FENG

Do you ever have times when you feel like Feng? He has thoughts that come into his head out of nowhere that he did something wrong. Feng worries that he cheated on his quiz. He knows that cheating is wrong, so he feels even more worried.

To push this worry away, Feng would normally tell his teacher and ask everyone around him if he actually cheated. But even when other people told him that he definitely didn't cheat, he just couldn't shake that thought. Poor Feng!

But Feng is able to stop his OCD loop by recognizing that this is just his OCD talking. He remembers how in the past his old way of asking others whether he did or didn't cheat just never seemed to work. So, this time, Feng simply notices his thought. He doesn't judge it. He doesn't say it's true. He doesn't say it's false. Feng feels the urge to ask his teacher and friends if he cheated, but he tries his best not to. And guess what happens? That pesky thought becomes a little weaker.

Remember: Thoughts are just thoughts, and they can only hurt us if we let them.

WATCHING CLOUDS

Below is a picture of some puffy clouds. Notice how some of them are big and others are small? In the clouds, write in some of the worries, thoughts, or doubts OCD makes you have.

Now, close your eyes. Imagine it's a windy day, but you can feel warm sunshine on your face. Light dances through tall, green trees. Now look up to the sky. So blue! So many big, puffy clouds. Like giant marshmallows filling the sky!

Try to imagine that the clouds are your OCD thoughts and worries. Just look at them. Don't say they should be there. Don't say they shouldn't be there. Just observe them as they slowly pass across the sky.

Onward and Upward

OCD often makes you do or say things over and over again. Remember what these are called? Compulsions—good job!

Kids with OCD do these things to make their scary or uncomfortable thoughts go away so they can feel better. For some kids, this might be repeating words, numbers, or prayers in a certain order or a certain number of times. For others, it might be counting objects in the room, like tiles on the ceiling or the corners on an object. OCD might also make kids press buttons on their computers, tablets, or video game controllers in an exact way or until it feels "just right."

Many times, OCD tells you that compulsions have certain "rules" that must be followed. And if you don't follow the rules, you have to start all over again.

Let's take a look at another story. This one is about Noor, who uses the "Test It Out" tool.

NOOR'S STORY

Noor is seven years old and has OCD. Sometimes Noor's OCD makes her touch, tap, or press things a certain way. For Noor, anything that twists, opens, clicks, switches, or unplugs can be really difficult for her and take up a lot of her time!

For example, even everyday items like a tablet, TV remote, or even a toothpaste cap can be hard to step away from. Each item has to be handled a certain way. The tablet needs to be plugged in until Noor hears the sound that she knows means it's charging. Sometimes this can take up to 10 minutes. Plug in. Beep. "Doesn't feel right." Unplug. "Let's try again." Plug in. Beep. "Mmm, not quite." Noor just can't seem to plug in the tablet and walk away.

Frustrated, Noor walks to the kitchen for a snack. The cookies are in a jar with a twisty lid. Noor has to twist and untwist the lid five times while counting in her head. But sometimes even after five times, she doubts herself and thinks, "Did I do it exactly five times? Better start again. One." Twist, untwist. "Two." Twist, untwist. Noor gets more and more frustrated. All she wants is a cookie! Just then, her uncle calls her from the other room to join him. "Noor, your favorite show is on." He's interrupted her twisting. Ugh.

Noor finishes her twisting and untwisting and starts to walk to the TV room. Usually, her OCD makes her do this while counting her steps out loud and touching the corners of the kitchen table on the way. But this time, she decides to face her OCD. Noor decides to be brave. Even though it makes her really uncomfortable, she tries to resist touching the kitchen table. She waits a whole 20 seconds but eventually feels the need to touch it. But this time, she decides to tap it out of order—right corner, left corner—and walks away.

Then, rather than counting her steps on the way to the TV room, Noor decides to say random numbers, letters, and even words as she walks. She even makes it a little silly. Left foot. "X." Right foot. "Seven hundred seventy-seven." Left foot. "Ketchup." Right foot. "Dandelion." As Noor keeps mixing up the rules of her OCD, she starts to worry a little less, even though it was hard in the beginning.

FEELING LIKE NOOR

Do you ever have times when you feel like Noor? She feels she needs to repeat things a certain way. Plugging and unplugging. Twisting and untwisting. Counting and recounting. With OCD, even everyday things can be difficult.

Did you notice that Noor doesn't have any specific worries or thoughts? Noor's OCD mostly has to do with compulsions. Remember, compulsions are things that OCD makes you do over and over again. Usually, this is to make scary or unwanted thoughts go away, but not always. Noor's OCD makes her feel she needs to follow very strict "rules."

But Noor is able to stop her OCD loop by breaking the rules. Even though Noor struggles in the beginning, she's able to face a part of her OCD in the end. This is super important to remember: Some is better than none.

Standing up to OCD takes time and is really hard work. So, even though Noor has to finish her first two compulsions—plugging and twisting—she's able to challenge her other compulsions. She should be proud of this. And even though it makes her nervous to not do the things OCD tells her she needs to do, she resists doing them anyway—on purpose. Noor is being really brave standing up to her OCD.

BE BRAVE LIKE NOOR

Think of all the things OCD tells you that you need to do or say or repeat. Is there something that you have to do in a particular order?

For example, Noor's OCD tells her that she needs to count her steps on the way to the TV room. To stand up to her OCD, Noor decides to mix things up. She breaks the rules—on purpose.

Look at the items below. In the shapes that look like bowling pins, write down all the "rules" your OCD tells you to follow. Now, in the shape that looks like a bowling ball, write down some ways you can break these rules. For example, you could just do the exact opposite.

Get creative or even silly, and knock those pins down.

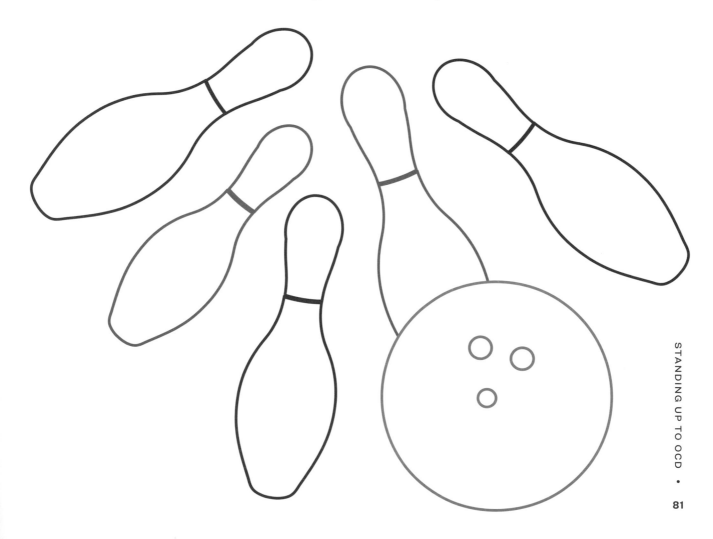

ALWAYS BE BRAVE,
BUT NEVER BE UNSAFE

You are being an absolute rock star! As you've already learned, it can be very hard to stand up to your OCD. As you continue climbing up and up your ladder, keep this in mind: Always be brave, but never be unsafe. This is extra important when you're using the "Test It Out" tool.

In general, the more you can stop yourself from doing the things OCD tells you that you need to do, the better. For example, if your OCD tells you to wash your hands every time you touch a doorknob, standing up to your OCD would be to not wash your hands. You might even go around purposely touching doorknobs, not washing your hands, and imagining something bad happening. This is all part of standing up to your OCD. Great job. Keep this up!

Keep in mind that you never want to do something that's dangerous and could actually hurt you or someone else. For example, let's say your OCD makes you worry about things getting "germy" from touching certain surfaces. Eating a piece of candy that was on the kitchen counter—that's okay. Eating a piece of candy that was on a dirty public bathroom floor—definitely not okay.

Or, imagine your OCD makes you worry about getting sick from eating certain foods. Eating a sandwich with turkey slices from a package with an expiration date two days away—that's okay. Eating raw or undercooked meat—definitely not okay.

Or, let's say your OCD makes you worry about accidentally harming someone else. Purposely thinking scary thoughts that you might hurt someone while using scissors—that's okay. Actually hurting someone in real life with scissors—definitely not okay.

Bring It On!

OCD can make scary thoughts come into your mind without warning. These thoughts are really difficult to have racing around in your brain, so, you try to push them away.

But what happens when you do that? Remember our hippopotamus example? When you try not to think about a hippopotamus in a bathing suit, what happens? That's right, that giant gray hippo wearing a silly swimsuit jumps into your mind.

What can you learn from this? Well, instead of pushing away the scary thoughts that OCD makes you have, you can try this: Purposely think about those thoughts. Bring them on! This may seem strange. Why would you want to think about bad things happening? The reason is: You want to teach your brain that thinking about something happening doesn't mean it will actually happen.

Let's imagine you really want your teacher to throw a party for your class tomorrow. How fun would that be? You want to have that party so badly, you start to think about it really, really, hard. You think of all the games and pizza and laughing and no homework. On and on you just keep imagining that you'll have a party tomorrow. You even say to yourself, "We're definitely having a party tomorrow. I just know it."

But stop for a moment and think: When you go to school tomorrow, are you any more likely to have a class party? Unfortunately, no. Another important thing to remember is that you're also no less likely to have a class party.

The point is this: Thinking about a class party in your mind is not the same as having a class party in real life.

The same is true for the thoughts and images and worries OCD might make you have. So, one way to stand up to your OCD is to purposely think of the scary things OCD tells you. Normally, you push these thoughts away and try your very best not to think of them. But this time, do the opposite. Bring on those thoughts! (Hint: It might be easiest to start at the bottom of your OCD ladder for this one.)

Let's look at a story about Suzanne.

SUZANNE'S STORY

Suzanne is nine years old and has OCD. Sometimes her OCD makes thoughts of getting sick pop in her head. One day, Suzanne is eating some popcorn. As she takes a handful, one of the kernels falls onto the carpet. Normally, she would throw it away. But this time, Suzanne wants to be brave. She picks up the kernel and pops it into her mouth. At first, she thinks, "Gross." But then she wonders, "What if I get sick? What if something bad happens?"

Suzanne ignores those thoughts because she knows that's her OCD talking. Normally, she would immediately go straight to the sink, wash her hands, ask her parents if she's okay, and tell herself she's clean and healthy. But not this time: Suzanne does the exact opposite of what her OCD wants.

Suzanne purposely thinks to herself, "Yup, I'm going to get sick." She feels her anxiety shoot up. But she doesn't back down. She brings those thoughts on! "That piece of popcorn was super germy. Now I'm germy. I will 100 percent absolutely, positively, definitely, for sure get sick." She notices her anxiety stays pretty high but goes down just a little bit.

Suzanne doesn't stop there. She even touches the carpet with her hand, gives her mom a hug, and thinks, "My mom is going to get sick. Yup, definitely happening. Mom is going to get sick." Over the next five minutes, Suzanne doesn't let herself give in. She doesn't say to herself that her hands are clean and there's no way her mom will get sick. Instead, she keeps saying to herself, "I have germs everywhere. I'm going to get sick. I'm going to get sick."

After doing this so, so, so many times, Suzanne notices her worries go down. She must have said, "I'm going to get sick," at least one hundred times, but the words have less power than they did before. Now they're just words!

FEELING LIKE SUZANNE

Do you ever have times when you feel like Suzanne? She feels worried that she'll catch germs and get herself and others sick. Normally, Suzanne's OCD makes her wash her hands and avoid things that she thinks have germs—like popcorn touching the floor.

But Suzanne is able to stop her OCD loop by purposely thinking of the bad thoughts. In the past, she'd normally push these scary thoughts away to make her feel less worried. Even though no one wants to get sick, Suzanne challenges herself. She starts to prove to herself that thinking about getting sick—even if she thinks about it really, really hard—doesn't mean she will. Wow, how brave is she?

BE BRAVE LIKE SUZANNE

Be like Suzanne—and be brave! Think of all the worries and thoughts and images that OCD makes pop into your head. Think of one that's not too hard—one lower down on your OCD ladder. Write down that thought in the space below. Even writing this thought down might give you a little anxiety, but that's okay.

Now, try to get even more brave. Write that thought down 10 more times. If you're feeling extra brave, you can even say it out loud as you write it. And if you're feeling super-duper brave, you can even think about that thing happening in real life.

At first, this might be really scary. But remember, your thoughts are just thoughts. Eventually, your brain gets bored. The more times you write and say and imagine your OCD thought, the less and less power it has over you. Amazing job. Way to be brave!

Even More Ways to Stand Up to OCD

Remember the story about Noor, and how she was able to stand up to her OCD by not doing the things OCD told her she needed to do? Sometimes, especially in the beginning, this can be very hard. That's why you should start with things near the bottom of your ladder. To help you out, here are a few more tricks you can try.

Use a timer: Let's say your OCD tells you to wash your hands when you have a thought of feeling dirty or "germy." Instead of washing your hands right away, try setting a timer to see how long you can go without washing your hands.

If it's still really hard, maybe try counting to 10 first. As you practice more and more, keep increasing the time. Next time, you could try 30 seconds. Then, one minute. Before you know it, you won't feel as worried and that urge to wash your hands won't feel so powerful.

Mix it up: What about when OCD tells you to do or say things in a certain order? Let's imagine it's dinner time. You'd like to sit down right away and start eating, but your OCD tells you to pull and push your chair three times, tap your dinner plate, and touch each piece of silverware.

To stand up to your OCD, you could change up the order. See what happens when you tap your dinner plate first, then pull and push your chair twice, and mix up the order of your silverware so you're doing it "wrong."

Reduce: This is similar to using a timer. But instead of increasing the time between your thoughts (obsessions) and actions (compulsions), you decrease the number of times or the amount of time you spend doing your compulsions.

Let's say your OCD makes you check that your pet's cage is closed five times. If trying to not check the cage at all—zero times—is too hard, try to check only four times. After some practice doing that, try decreasing the number of times you check even more. Eventually, work your way down to zero.

Remember, even if you don't reach zero times, you're still doing less than what your OCD tells you to do. And that's still something to be very proud of.

Leave: Let's say your OCD gets you "stuck" on checking that your toys in your room are arranged in a certain order. If you notice that you're getting "stuck" on counting, checking, or ordering your toys, try your best to leave the room. Walk away if you can. For a little extra help, try saying to yourself, "I know this is my OCD making me check. Even though this feels uncomfortable and I really want to keep checking, I'm going to see what happens if I try leaving. I can do this."

Ask for help: It'll be super helpful to talk to an adult in the house about what they can do when they notice you're getting "stuck" in an OCD loop. For some kids, it might be a parent giving encouragement when they're using the "Test It Out" tool: "You've gone three minutes without checking. Great job!" For other kids, it might be an aunt gently helping them walk away when they're "stuck" in the middle of a compulsion: "Let's step away from the refrigerator and out of the kitchen. How about you follow me outside? I know your OCD is getting you stuck, but let's just see what happens if we walk away."

Try using these tips to help you face your OCD. You can use more than one of these tricks at the same time. Remember, the more you can resist doing your compulsions, the better—whether it's the amount of times you do them, or how long you do them, or mixing up the order of how you do them.

Resisting your compulsions will make you feel uncomfortable, and maybe even scared. Those are difficult feelings to have. After all, who wants to feel that way? Just know that those feelings are also a sign that what you're doing is working. It means you're standing up to your OCD, and you're not giving in to what your OCD says. Keep practicing and keep being brave. That uncomfortable or scared feeling will get a little smaller each time.

USING YOUR NEW TOOLS

Write down some of your compulsions on the lines below. Remember, these are the things that OCD tells you that you need to do again and again.

Now, look at the tools on pages 87 and 88. How could you use these tools to resist one of your compulsions? For example, is there a way you could use a timer or mix up the order of your compulsions? Write down how you might do this.

TIME TO LOOK AT YOUR ACHIEVEMENTS!

You're doing an amazing job so far. Using all of the tools you've learned is something to be proud of.

Sometimes, it can help to redraw your OCD ladder to see how much progress you've made. Think of all the things OCD tells you are scary. Remember, these can be thoughts that don't make sense that come into your head and won't leave you alone. These can also be things you feel you need to say or do again and again.

Write the hard things at the very top of your ladder. Write things that are less hard in the middle. Keep going until you reach the bottom of the ladder.

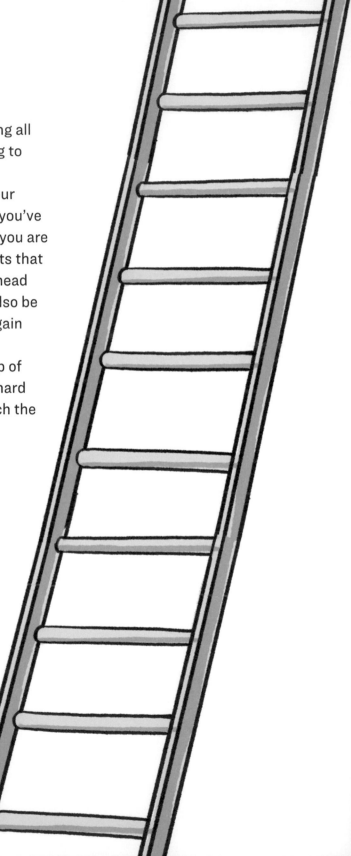

Take a good look at your new ladder. Do you see anything that surprises you? Maybe there's something at the bottom of the ladder that used to be at the top of the ladder. It used to be really hard, but now it's a lot easier. Maybe something that used to be scary or hard isn't even on the ladder anymore.

As you continue practicing, redraw your ladder from time to time. This way you can see the things that still bother you—things you might want to keep working on.

Redrawing your ladder also shows you where you've made progress. That can give you a boost of encouragement. Things that used to be at the very top of the ladder might be a little further down now. That shows you've been working really hard. You should feel proud of yourself.

You've Made Excellent Progress!

Wonderful job so far! You've been practicing really hard to stand up to your OCD.

In this chapter, you drew your OCD ladder and started making some great progress climbing it, using all the tools you've learned. Hopefully you can see how your ladder has started to change. Things that used to be at the very top of the ladder might seem a little easier now. Things that used to be at the bottom of the ladder might not even be there anymore. Keep on climbing!

In the final chapter, you're going to learn even more tools. These tips and tricks are going to be helpful not just for dealing with OCD, but also for other feelings like sadness, worry, or stress. Let's get going!

CHAPTER 4

KEEP STANDING TALL, EVEN IF YOU FALL

So far, you've learned a lot about your OCD. You've become an expert OCD detective and have already been practicing tips and tricks to help you stand up to your OCD. Great work! Now, the most important part is that you keep practicing. You've done an awesome job, so just keep at it.

It's important to know that it's completely normal if there are times when your OCD comes back and gets a little worse. No need to panic. It doesn't mean you're back at square one. Think of all the progress you've made and all the skills you've learned. These will always be with you and nothing can take them away. Just like a car needs a tune-up once in a while to run better, you might need a tune-up to work on your OCD.

In this last chapter, you're going to learn how to spot when it's time for a tune-up. You're also going to learn about even more tools you can add to your toolbox. And these tools aren't just for OCD. They can be helpful for many other feelings you might have, like when you're feeling sad, nervous, or just stressed out. Let's check them out.

An Introduction to Thinking Traps

Remember how you learned that your feelings, thoughts, and actions are connected? Because they're connected, how you think about things can have a really big impact on how you feel. And everyone's thoughts are different. This means that kids can have different thoughts about the same event.

Let's say you're walking to class and you see your best friend down the hallway. It's time for recess, so the hallways are pretty busy and noisy. Your friend is talking with some of your other classmates. As you walk by, you wave hello. But your friend doesn't wave back. Your friend just keeps on walking.

What are some possible reasons why your friend didn't wave back?

Let's look at three different stories from three different kids about why their best friends didn't wave back.

CHRIS'S STORY

Chris waves to his best friend, but his friend doesn't wave back. Chris gets a little upset and thinks to himself, "Why won't he wave back? How rude. Best friends should always say hello to each other in the hallway, and now he's ignoring me—on purpose!" Chris gets angrier and decides not to play with his friend at recess.

PERRY'S STORY

Perry waves to his best friend, but his friend doesn't wave back. Perry gets a little sad and thinks to himself, "Why won't he wave back? Oh no! What if I did something wrong? He must be mad at me. It's all my fault." Perry gets anxious and worries to himself, "What if no one likes me? I don't have any friends. This is terrible!"

ROSIE'S STORY

Rosie waves to her best friend, but her friend doesn't wave back. Rosie is a little bit surprised, but immediately thinks to herself, "It's really noisy in the hallway right now and she was talking to some other classmates. She probably just didn't notice me." Rosie continues walking to recess and thinks about how excited she is to play with her friends.

WHY DIDN'T THEY WAVE BACK?

Wow, such different stories! Can you see how even though it's the same event—a friend not waving back—each kid has a different way of thinking about it? Each kid comes up with their own reasons for why their best friend didn't wave back. Chris thinks his friend is being mean and ignoring him on purpose. Perry thinks he did something wrong and that nobody likes him.

But look at Rosie. She just plays it cool. She thinks of all the possible reasons why her friend didn't wave back. She remembers that it's pretty loud and hallways can get busy, so maybe her friend just didn't see her. Rosie doesn't think bad things about her friend, and she also doesn't think bad things about herself. She doesn't blame other people, and she also doesn't blame herself. Rosie is thinking in a balanced way.

The truth is, if they don't ask, none of the kids can really know for sure why their friend didn't wave back. It's possible that Chris is right that his friend is being rude on purpose. Perry might be right that he did something wrong that upset his friend and everyone is mad at him.

Now, stop and think for a minute. If someone is your best friend, why would they ignore you on purpose? Is that what best friends do? And even if Perry did do something to upset his friend, does it make sense to think that no one likes him?

Remember, how you think about something can have a really powerful effect on how you feel. Sometimes, when our feelings change, it's because our thinking has changed. Sometimes our thinking isn't balanced. When this happens, our minds might fall into a thinking trap. The next section is going to teach you all about these traps.

Don't Think Negative, Don't Think Positive—Just Think Balanced

To think more balanced, it's important to get really good at spotting thinking traps. They can be pretty sneaky. There are many types of thinking traps, and you're going to learn about a few of them.

As you practice learning to become an expert thinking trap spotter, you'll also get better at changing your thoughts so they're a bit more balanced. You already have a lot of practice doing this from using the "Thought Changer" tool. You can also work on changing thoughts that aren't OCD. Remember, you are in control of your thoughts. And you have the power to change them. It just takes a little practice.

Keep in mind that the goal of balanced thinking is not to think 100 percent positive. Does this sound a little strange? You might have heard your parents, teachers, or friends say, "Think on the bright side," or, "Just think positive." While many times we do want to think *more* positive, we don't want to think *all* positive.

For example, let's say you failed a quiz. What a bummer. On the one hand, you don't want to think negative. Saying things like, "I'm so stupid," and, "I'm a failure at everything," isn't very helpful. But you also don't want to think too positive. Saying things like, "Yay! I got an F. This is awesome!" is also not very helpful. Getting an F is a total bummer. Of course you might feel a little down.

Like a seesaw, we want our thinking to be somewhere in the middle, not at either end. We need to think things through and take in all the facts—like a detective would. So, a more balanced thought might be, "Geez. An F. Not my best grade, but I can certainly bring it up. I'll study harder for the next exam. I can do this."

In the next section, you're going to meet two friends: Tony the Thinking Trapper and Betty the Balanced Thinker. As you read, notice how Tony isn't thinking in a very balanced way. He falls into a different thinking trap every time. Luckily, Betty is there to help him out.

Let's go through each thinking trap and find out how to change it.

ZEBRA THINKING

What color are zebras? Right! They're black and white. The zebra thinking trap happens when we think in extremes. We see things as either all black or all white. The problem with thinking like this is that it misses all the shades of gray in between. Black and white are not the only two colors. There are many colors. (A clever kid once called this the "grainbow"—as in, the "shades-of-gray" rainbow.)

Our thoughts are much more complicated than a zebra's stripes. When we fall into the zebra thinking trap, if something isn't perfect, we think it's terrible. We see ourselves as a failure. This is also called "all-or-nothing thinking."

Here's an example of how Tony falls into the zebra thinking trap:

Tony the Thinking Trapper: "I used the 'Test It Out' tool and was able to resist my compulsion to wash my hands for almost the whole day. There was one time I struggled and couldn't stop myself. I failed the entire day. Why did I even bother practicing?"

Do you see how Tony is thinking in black-and-white terms? Even though he did a great job standing up to his OCD for almost the entire day, he thinks his effort was all for nothing because he struggled just one time.

Let's see how Betty would change this thought to be more balanced:

Betty the Balanced Thinker: "I was able to stand up to my OCD for almost the entire day. That's something to be proud of. Even though I struggled a little, it was only one time. That doesn't mean I failed. The practice I put in was still worth it. I can try again tomorrow and see how I do."

NOW IT'S YOUR TURN!

Can you help Tony not fall into the zebra thinking trap?

Below is a picture of Tony and Betty. See how there's a blank bubble next to Betty? Write something in the bubble that Betty could say to help Tony cheer up and think in a more balanced way. For example, maybe Betty could say something like, "You were still able to stand up to your OCD. You didn't fail anything. You did a really good job today and you should be proud, Tony."

"SHOULD, MUST, HAVE TO"

Have you ever heard someone say, "should've, could've, would've"? This type of thinking trap is similar to that. "Should, must, have to" thinking happens when we make up strict rules about how we think things "should" be or how we expect them to be.

The problem with thinking this way is that if we don't meet these rules or fall short, we get upset. Sometimes we use the words "should," "must," "have to," or need to when we really mean "want to."

Here's an example of how Tony falls into the "should, must, have to" thinking trap:

Tony the Thinking Trapper: "I have to practice standing up to my OCD at least two hours a day. If I don't, I failed."

Do you see how Tony is setting up the rule that he needs to practice at least two hours a day? It's great to want to practice, because it's how you get better. But by saying to himself that he has to practice a certain amount of time, Tony is putting all of the power in a made-up rule. What you want to do is put the power in you.

Remember, it's sometimes best to switch out the word "have" to with "want" to. Just this tiny word change can make a huge difference.

Now let's see what Betty might say:

Betty the Balanced Thinker: "I want to practice standing up to my OCD 2 hours a day. But even if I don't reach 2 hours, some practice is better than none."

NOW IT'S YOUR TURN!

It's your turn to help Tony out. Can you help Tony not fall into the "should, must, have to" thinking trap? In the bubble next to Betty, write in something she could say to help Tony cheer up and think in a more balanced way.

LABELING

Why do clothing and food have labels? That's right: A label tells you what something is. But people are very complicated, so it doesn't make sense to use one or two words to describe a person.

The labeling thinking trap happens when we use a negative, mean, or extreme word to describe something we did wrong or that someone else did wrong. The problem with thinking this way is that it makes us feel bad. Even worse, it doesn't lead to any positive or helpful changes.

Here's an example of how Tony falls into the labeling thinking trap:

Tony the Thinking Trapper: "I just can't seem to stop locking and unlocking this door. This is so frustrating. Geez, I'm so weird."

Do you see how Tony is labeling himself as "weird"? That's a really mean thing to say to himself. Do you think talking that way to himself is going to make him get unstuck any faster? Probably not. If anything, it'll probably make Tony more "stuck."

What would Betty say about this same situation?

Betty the Balanced Thinker: "I just can't seem to stop locking and unlocking this door. This is pretty frustrating. But doors are high up on my OCD ladder, so it makes sense that this would be hard. I need to be patient with myself. Just because I'm stuck doesn't mean I'm weird or stupid. It just means I have OCD, which I'm working really hard on."

NOW IT'S YOUR TURN!

You're up again. Can you help Tony not fall into the labeling thinking trap? Write something in the bubble that Betty could say to help Tony cheer up and think in a more balanced way.

EMOTIONAL REASONING

The emotional reasoning trap is sort of complicated, so let's break it down. The word *emotional* refers to emotions, or feelings. The word reasoning refers to explaining why we think about something a certain way (our reasons for thinking that way). So, emotional reasoning happens when we use our feelings to explain something instead of using facts. The problem is that our feelings don't always make sense and can sometimes be wrong.

Here's an example of how Tony falls into the emotional reasoning trap:

Tony the Thinking Trapper: "I'm trying really hard to resist saying my nighttime prayers in a certain order. I'm super anxious. That probably means I won't be able to do it. I might as well just give in."

Do you see how Tony is already thinking he won't be able to stand up to his OCD, just because he's feeling anxious?

Betty has something to say about this.

Betty the Balanced Thinker: "I'm trying really hard to resist saying my nighttime prayers in a certain order. I'm super anxious. But standing up to my OCD is supposed to make me anxious. That's how it works. And I've been anxious more times than I can count standing up to my OCD, but I always end up just fine. It's never, ever as bad as I think it's going to be. Plus, most of the time, I actually beat my fear. So, chances are that even though I'm really nervous, I'll probably be able to do this. I'm not going to give in. I've got this."

NOW IT'S YOUR TURN!

You know the drill. Can you help Tony not fall into the emotional reasoning trap? Write something in the bubble that Betty could say to help Tony cheer up and think in a more balanced way.

BINOCULAR TRICK

What happens when you look in a pair of binoculars? That's right, things that are far in the distance become much larger. The binocular trick happens when we make something a much bigger deal than it actually is. We think things are way, way worse than they really are.

But have you ever looked through binoculars the wrong way? Instead of getting big, things in the distance become really small. So, we can also use the binocular trick to change something into a much smaller deal.

Here's an example of how Tony falls into the binocular trick thinking trap:

Tony the Thinking Trapper: "Today I keep getting stuck on counting everything in threes. I'm never going to get better. I'm going to be stuck with OCD for the rest of my life. No one is going to want to be my friend. I'll never get a job. Everything is going to be terrible. And I'll never, ever be happy."

Do you see how Tony goes from getting "stuck" on counting in threes to saying he'll never, ever be happy? That's quite a jump.

How does Betty use the binocular trick?

Betty the Balanced Thinker: "Today I keep getting stuck on counting everything in threes. It's tough, but that doesn't mean I'll never get better. In fact, I've already seen some improvement. Counting in threes used to get me stuck for hours at a time. Now, I can get unstuck in minutes, and sometimes I don't get stuck at all. OCD can get hard at times, but I know I'm going in the right direction."

NOW IT'S YOUR TURN!

Time to give Tony some help. Can you help Tony not fall into the binocular trick thinking trap? Write something in the bubble that Betty could say to help Tony cheer up and think in a more balanced way.

MIND READING

Can you read someone else's mind? Unless you're a magical psychic, you can never really know what someone's thinking. The mind reading thinking trap happens when we think we know 100 percent of what someone else is thinking. When we fall into this trap, we jump to the conclusion that something's bad without checking to find out if that's really true. This thinking trap is super important and is probably the most common trap we all fall into.

Here's an example of how Tony falls into the mind reading thinking trap:

Tony the Thinking Trapper: "I'm stuck clicking the remote on and off and on and off. I hear my mom laughing in the other room. She's probably laughing at me. She thinks my OCD is so weird. I bet she thinks I'm weird, too."

Do you see how when Tony hears his mother laughing, he thinks she's laughing at him? And he's sure his mom thinks he's weird. Poor Tony.

Help us out, Betty!

Betty the Balanced Thinker: "I'm stuck clicking the remote on and off and on and off. I hear my mom laughing in the other room. I know she's having a dinner party with her friends. And they're always laughing and telling jokes. She's probably just having a good time with her friends. I'm sure the laughing has nothing to do with me."

NOW IT'S YOUR TURN!

Tony needs assistance. Can you help Tony not fall into the mind reading thinking trap? Write something in the bubble that Betty could say to help Tony cheer up and think in a more balanced way.

FORTUNE TELLING

Can you see into the future? Unless you have superpowers, you can never know for sure what will happen in the future. The fortune telling thinking trap happens when we think we can know the future, as though we have a magic crystal ball. And sometimes we think something bad is going to happen even though there's no way we can know if it will.

Here's an example of how Tony falls into the fortune telling thinking trap:

Tony the Thinking Trapper: "Scary thoughts about hurting other people keep popping into my head. I wish they'd stop. I'm going to have these thoughts forever. My OCD is never going to get better."

Do you see how Tony is sure that his OCD will never get better? But what evidence does he have? How can he know this for certain?

Let's see what Betty thinks.

Betty the Balanced Thinker: "Scary thoughts about hurting other people keep popping into my head. I want them to stop, and I'm working on it. Just because I have OCD now doesn't mean I'll never get better. These types of scary thoughts used to be at the very top of my OCD ladder. Now they're halfway down the ladder. So, the thought of me never getting better just isn't true. I'm doing great and am going to keep working hard."

NOW IT'S YOUR TURN!

Your turn again. Can you help Tony not fall into the fortune telling thinking trap? Write something in the bubble that Betty could say to help Tony cheer up and think in a more balanced way.

"YEAH, BUT"

The "yeah, but" thinking trap happens when we think good things that happen don't matter. Even if something positive happens, we reject it and say it wasn't good enough. This is also called the "doesn't count" mistake.

Here's an example of how Tony falls into the "yeah, but" thinking trap:

Tony the Thinking Trapper: "My grandfather says I'm making really good progress. He told me that I used to wash my hands over 50 times a day. Now I'm down to 10 times. Yeah, but so what? Ten times is still a lot. And there are so many other parts of my OCD that haven't gotten better."

Do you see how Tony is focusing on the things he hasn't done instead of the things he has done?

Let's see what Betty thinks.

Betty the Balanced Thinker: "My grandfather says I'm making really good progress. He's right. I used to wash my hands over 50 times a day. Now I'm down to just 10 times. That's 80 percent less—wow! I should be proud of myself for that. I know there are still a lot of other parts of my OCD I need to work on, but I've already proven to myself that the more I practice, the easier it gets."

NOW IT'S YOUR TURN!

Your assistance is needed. Can you help Tony not fall into the "yeah, but" thinking trap? Write something in the bubble that Betty could say to help Tony cheer up and think in a more balanced way.

INK IN THE BEAKER

What happens when you take a drop of ink, plop it in a beaker of water, and give it a good swirl? That's right, everything goes from clear to dark. Just like the ink changes the color of the water, the ink in the beaker thinking trap happens when we let one thing change how we see everything else. If one bad thing happens, we think everything is bad.

Here's an example of how Tony falls into the ink in the beaker thinking trap:

Tony the Thinking Trapper: "It's been a whole week without having any OCD problems. But today, I had my old compulsion come back of asking my mom, 'Are you sure?' over and over. My OCD is just as bad as it was in the beginning. I'm back at square one. This week is awful."

Do you see how Tony is saying his entire week is awful just because his OCD returned for only one day?

How might Betty help us out?

Betty the Balanced Thinker: "It's been a whole week without having any OCD problems. Today, I had my old habit come back of asking my mom 'Are you sure?' over and over. This is one of my compulsions. It stinks that my OCD has come back a bit, but I know how to stand up to it. Just because today is a little tough doesn't mean my whole week is ruined. I still had an entire week without OCD problems, and that's something to celebrate."

NOW IT'S YOUR TURN!

You're an expert at this by now! Can you help Tony not fall into the ink in the beaker thinking trap? Write something in the bubble that Betty could say to help Tony cheer up and think in a more balanced way.

BLAMING

Sometimes, things are our fault and we should apologize for them. Other times, things aren't our fault. The blaming thinking trap happens when we take responsibility for things that aren't our fault. The problem with this trap is that it can make us think we're the cause of bad things happening that have nothing to do with us.

Here's an example of how Tony falls into the blaming thinking trap:

Tony the Thinking Trapper: "I hear my parents arguing in the other room. I bet it's because they're stressed because of me always asking them questions and getting stuck on counting. I'm the one with OCD, so it's my fault they're arguing."

Do you see how Tony is blaming himself for his parents arguing? He doesn't actually know why they're arguing, but he blames himself anyway.

Betty, we could use a little help.

Betty the Balanced Thinker: "I hear my parents arguing in the other room. I'm not sure why they're arguing. But they've never once told me they're upset with me because I have OCD, so I doubt that's why. Sometimes parents just argue."

NOW IT'S YOUR TURN!

Tony needs your support one more time. Can you help Tony not fall into the blaming thinking trap? Write something in the bubble that Betty could say to help Tony cheer up and think in a more balanced way.

You're a Thinking Trap Expert!

Great job so far. Hopefully by now you've got a really good understanding of thinking traps. When you notice a change in how you're feeling, go back to this list of thinking traps. Does your thinking match one (or more) of these traps? If so, try to think of a more balanced thought.

Remember, the goal isn't to think negatively or positively. Instead, the goal is to think somewhere in the middle. Look at the facts—just like a good detective would. The more you practice, the easier it'll get.

LEARN MORE ABOUT YOUR THINKING TRAPS

Here is a chart with five columns: date/time, action/event, feelings, thoughts, and traps. Over the next few days, try to be extra aware of changes in how you feel. This could be any feeling, like worry, anger, or sadness.

Whenever you notice a change in how you feel, write down:

1. **The date and time**
2. **The action/event, like where you were or what happened**
3. **How you felt**
4. **What you were thinking**
5. **If there is one, the name of the thinking trap you fell into**

If there's more than one feeling, thought, or trap, write them down, too. Remember, your thoughts, feelings, and actions are all connected.

As you fill in more and more rows, look to see if you notice any patterns. What thinking traps seem to pop up again and again? Then, go back and see if you can be like Betty and make some of your thoughts more balanced. Some examples have been filled in to get you started.

DATE/TIME	ACTION/ EVENT	FEELING(S)	THOUGHT(S)	TRAP(S)
August 8th, 3:00 p.m.	Lost soccer game	Frustrated, Sad	"It's my fault the team lost. I'm a terrible goalie."	Blaming, Labeling
August 9th, 9:00 a.m.	Erased and rewrote answers for a quiz over and over	Stressed, Frustrated	"I'm so strange. All that time was wasted, and I probably failed."	Labeling, Fortune telling

BE SPECIFIC, SPECIFIC, SPECIFIC!

You've done an amazing job learning about thinking traps. You now have a helpful skill that you can use wherever you are.

When you stand up to OCD, things can get pretty hard. An important tip to remember is that when something bad or negative happens, be specific. For example, if you fail a test, then just say, "I failed a test," not, "I'm a failure." If you lost a basketball game, then just say, "I lost a basketball game," not, "I'm a terrible athlete."

The same is true for your OCD. If you're "stuck" doing a compulsion that seems strange, it's okay to think to yourself that the action is strange, but you are not strange. If an odd obsession pops into your head, it's okay to think to yourself that the thought is odd, but you are not odd.

Remember, be specific, specific, specific!

Be Kind to Yourself

Having OCD can be so difficult. And standing up to your OCD takes a lot of work. All those worries, doubts, repeating, and thinking "what if" can get you down. Sometimes, kids are even mean to themselves. It's very important to look out for this and catch yourself thinking this way.

Let's look at a story about Aiden, who's frustrated that he's struggling with his OCD.

AIDEN'S STORY

Aiden is 10 years old and has OCD. His OCD makes him check doors very often. Sometimes, Aiden gets "stuck" and can't walk away until he opens and closes the door until it feels "just right." Closet doors are lowest on Aiden's OCD ladder, and he's already done really well closing these just once and being able to walk away. Now he's tackling his bedroom door, which is higher on his OCD ladder. Aiden tries to close the door only one time but has a scary thought pop into his head. He tries not to open his bedroom door again but is having a difficult time. He opens and closes and opens and closes the door. Aiden starts to get frustrated. He says to himself, "I just can't stop. I hate OCD. I can't even close a door and walk away. I'm so dumb. I'm so weird. I'm never, ever going to get better!"

FEELING LIKE AIDEN

Do you ever have times when you feel like Aiden? He's working so hard climbing his OCD ladder but gets "stuck" on opening and closing his bedroom door. Are you able to spot some of the thinking traps Aiden falls into? That's right! Aiden is labeling ("I'm so weird") and fortune telling ("I'm never, ever going to get better!"). Way to catch those.

Now imagine if instead of talking to himself, Aiden would talk to his best friend Angel that same way.

AIDEN AND ANGEL

Aiden and Angel are best friends. They always hang out, sit together at lunch, and play video games. One day after school, Aiden and Angel are studying for a math quiz. They often help each other out when one of them doesn't understand something. Angel needs help on a long division problem and asks, "Hey I don't get this part. Can you help me?" Aiden says, "Why don't you understand this? This is so easy. It's just division. You're so stupid. You're a loser. You're going to fail tomorrow."

Do you think Aiden and Angel would stay friends? Probably not. Aiden is being really mean to Angel. Is that how you treat your best friend? Do you yell at them, call them names, and tell them they're going to fail? Of course not. As a friend, you're supportive, patient, and kind. You talk nicely to them. You give them encouragement. You build them up, not tear them down. This is also how you should treat yourself.

This can be a good way to check if you're being kind to yourself: If you wouldn't speak that way to a friend, you probably shouldn't speak that way to yourself.

Let's see what it would look like if Aiden could be a little more kind to himself.

AIDEN THE BALANCED THINKER

"This is really frustrating. But I need to remember that bedroom doors are higher on my ladder, so it makes sense this would be hard. Just because I didn't do as well as I wanted to today, it doesn't mean I won't do good things later. I just ran into a road bump and these things happen. When I learned to play piano, I was really struggling, especially when I was playing a harder song. And there were some days when I did better than others. But the more and more I practiced, the easier it got. The same is true for my OCD. There are going to be some good days, but there are also going to be some hard days. I've just got to keep practicing. I can do this."

Do you see how Aiden is able to be a little nicer to himself? He reminds himself that standing up to his OCD is tough work. He thinks of other difficult things he's done in the past that took a lot of practice. He thinks in a balanced way and gives himself a little boost of encouragement. Remember, if you wouldn't speak that way to a friend, you're probably being too hard on yourself. Check your thinking and be kind to yourself.

A LITTLE KINDNESS GOES A LONG WAY

Below is a picture of Hannah surrounded by a lot of thought bubbles. She's having a really hard time. Hannah is feeling pretty anxious and thinking very negative. Sometimes, she's just plain mean to herself.

Let's help Hannah out. See how each thought bubble has a blank one next to it? Think about what you might say to her. What encouragement can you give her? How can you help Hannah think more balanced and be a little more kind to herself? How might you respond to Hannah in the blank bubble?

WHEN OCD MAKES YOU FEEL BLUE

Having OCD can be really, really hard. When uncomfortable thoughts pop into your head, when you keep repeating things and just can't stop—OCD can feel like a mountain you'll never be able to climb. Standing up to your OCD can be really tiring. Sometimes it feels like it's just too much to handle. Sometimes kids feel like giving up. And sometimes kids feel sad.

It's okay to feel sad.

Sometimes when we get sad, it's because we're having sad thoughts. Be sure to catch yourself to make sure you aren't falling into any thinking traps! You already have a ton of practice changing these to be more balanced. There are also other things you can do when you're feeling sad that can help.

Take off the blue glasses. You already have a head start doing this. When we get sad, many times it's because we're seeing things as all negative, as if we're wearing big, blue glasses that make everything seem bad. Try to notice what you're thinking when you're feeling down. How could you challenge that thought to be more balanced? Remember, the goal isn't to put on shiny, pink glasses and see everything as wonderful. Just take off the blue ones and see things as they actually are.

Exercise. This is really important. Getting your body moving is a very helpful way to feel better. When have you ever exercised and came back feeling in a worse mood than when you started? Probably not often. Try to exercise at least three days a week for at least 20 minutes to feel a mood boost.

Schedule activities. When we get sad, sometimes it's because we're not doing enough with our days. You probably won't feel better sitting inside a dark room for weeks at a time, not seeing friends, and not doing fun things. It can help to make a list of all the things you enjoy. Try to do a few of these every day, even if they're small things.

Eat healthy. Your diet can have a big impact on your mood. Try to cut down on junk food and eat a balanced diet.

Reach out for support. When we're going through a hard time, leaning on others for support is really important. Be sure to ask teachers, coaches, friends, and family for help when you need it. Even if it's not to talk about your feelings, just spending time with someone you care about can be helpful.

How to Relax and Stay in the Here and Now

You've learned so much about how to think more balanced and change your thoughts. Now, let's change gears a bit and learn some different types of skills. You can use these tools almost anywhere, and they can help calm you down if you're feeling worried, angry, or stressed.

Remember, just like everything else you've learned so far, these will take some practice. Don't give up if you don't see progress right away. Just like playing a sport or learning an instrument, it's important to keep practicing to see the benefits. Keep it up!

DROP YOUR ANCHOR

Do you have a time machine? Are you able to go back and change the past? What about a crystal ball? Are you able to peek ahead and see the future?

Wouldn't that be exciting? It's not possible to go back in time. It's not possible to go forward in time.

But even though we can't flash backward or forward, sometimes your mind gets "stuck." It can get "stuck" on thinking about things we should or shouldn't have done in the past. It can also get "stuck" thinking about things that may or may not happen in the future. When your mind gets "stuck" like this, many times we get sad or worried.

But like we've said, there's no high-tech time machine, and there's no magic crystal ball. The more we try to control these things, the more we get upset. So, if we can't change the past or know the future, what can we do?

One strategy is to practice getting really good at being in the present moment. This means you learn to just watch and observe everything happening around you and inside you.

Focus on the here and now. Do this without judging. You don't say things should be there. You don't say things shouldn't be there. This includes everything from thoughts and feelings to sounds and objects. (Hint: You have a little practice with this from using the "Observer" tool from the last chapters, too.)

What does an anchor do? That's right! It holds a ship firmly in place. When we talk about anchoring for people, we mean the same thing. Sometimes our minds can be like storms—lots of intense worries, fears, sadness, or anger.

But we don't try to fight the storm, make it go away, or say it shouldn't be there. Instead, when we use an anchoring skill, we hold firmly. We just observe. We don't let the storm shake us. And eventually, the storm passes.

Activity *continued*

There are many ways to anchor yourself. One easy way is to use your senses. Let's try it out.

First, what are some things you can see in the room? This could be a person, plant, picture on the wall, or any other type of object. Name a few.

Now close your eyes. Turn your attention to sounds. What are some things you can hear in the room? This could be someone else talking, your breathing, the gentle hum of a fan, maybe a bird chirping—anything. Name a few.

Next, focus on your body. What are some things you can feel, either with your hands, on your body, or inside you? This could be a surface you can touch nearby, the feeling of your feet firmly against the ground, the clothes on your body, or your heart beating in your chest. Name a few.

Now, are there things you can smell? If so, name them.

SET SAIL!

Imagine that you're a boat at sea. There's a storm brewing! Do you see the puffy, dark storm clouds on the previous page? What about the crackling lightning? And those crashing waves? That's quite a storm! In the pictures of the clouds, lightning, and waves, write down some of your worries and negative feelings.

Now look at the big anchor on the boat. That will hold you steady. Let's practice the anchoring skill you just learned. First, find a comfortable place. Make sure you're sitting and relaxed. Take a few deep breaths. Now, what are things you can see in the room? Take your time. Get a good look at everything around you. Try to find things you may not normally notice. Name at least five.

Now, with your eyes closed, try to name all the things you can hear. Take your time and really try to notice even the quietest of things.

Next, with your eyes still closed, what about things you feel? Scan your body from your toes to your head. Take note of any feelings, tension, or textures. Finally, take a deep breath. Do you notice any smells? If so, can you describe them? If not, take another deep breath and focus on how your lungs fill up just like a balloon.

Slowly open your eyes.

TAKE A DEEP BREATH

Another helpful tool that is always with you is your breath. Focusing on slowing your breathing can be a great way to calm your body down.

For this, you want to breathe in slowly and have your belly fill up just like a balloon. It helps if you put one hand on your chest and the other hand on your belly. Unlike normal everyday breathing, when you take a deep breath, the hand on your belly should come out more than the hand on your chest.

LET'S PRACTICE!

First, breathe out all the air through your mouth. Next, breathe in slowly and deeply through your nose. Do this and hold for about seven seconds. Now, slowly breathe out of your mouth. Do this for about five to eight seconds and be sure to breathe all of the air out. Keep repeating. A good rule to remember is that your breathing out should last about twice as long as your breathing in.

When you're doing this, your mind might wander. That's okay. Just observe your thoughts, whatever they might be, and try to bring your attention back to your breathing. Imagine your thoughts are just like clouds drifting across the sky. Notice them, then bring your attention back to your breathing.

TENSE YOUR MUSCLES

One more helpful tool is to tense and relax each muscle group in your body. You start with your toes and work your way up your body all the way to your face. You practice squeezing each muscle group for 5 to 10 seconds, then release.

What's nice about this skill is that you can do it anywhere. And when you get really good at it, you can just tense all your muscles at once, release, and repeat. You can also just do your toes, legs, abdomen, arms, and fists without anyone evening noticing!

LET'S PRACTICE!

First, find a quiet place where you won't be bothered. This could be a comfy chair or couch. Start with your toes. Curl them tightly for 5 to 10 seconds, then slowly release. Notice the feeling of warmth and relaxation as you let go.

Next, lift up both of your legs straight out and press your knees together. Tense a few seconds. Hold it, and release.

Now, tighten your abdomen. To do this, imagine you're pulling your stomach toward your back. Tense, hold, and release. Move to your chest. Take a long, deep breath, puff your belly out, and hold for 10 seconds.

Next, take both of your hands and tightly squeeze them to make two fists. Hold for a few seconds, then very slowly release each hand, focusing on the warmth and tension leaving your fingertips. For your neck, tilt your head all the way back while arching your back so your chest puffs out. Hold and release.

Now, shrug your shoulders as high as you can, as if you're trying to reach your ears. Keep them there for a few seconds. Slowly release.

Finally, for your face, close your eyes tightly, bite down, push your lips together, and point your chin down. Tense all these muscles, hold, and release.

WHEN YOU CAN'T FOCUS OR STOP TWITCHING

We all have trouble concentrating from time to time. But some kids with OCD really struggle with this. They might have a hard time focusing in class. They might talk out of turn or find it difficult to stop interrupting. They might be overly active and hyper for long periods of time. They might struggle with sitting still and seem to forget things.

Some kids with OCD also make sudden movements that look really "jerky." For example, this could be squinting their eyes, whipping their head, twitching their nose, or popping their shoulder. Some kids also make sudden noises. These could be things like clearing their throat, sniffing, or making squeaking sounds.

If one or both of these things sound like you, it might be helpful to grab a parent and take a look at the Resources section at the back of this book for more helpful information on these.

THE BENEFITS OF STAYING STRONG

You've learned a lot about how your thoughts can affect your feelings and actions. Since that's the case, thinking positive or saying encouraging things can make you feel better and stay motivated.

Sometimes it helps to see these things written down when we really need a boost of encouragement. In the space below, jot down a few things you can say to yourself when the going gets tough so you can stay strong against your OCD.

For example, what are some positive things about continuing to stand up to your OCD? How would your life be different? Why might it be good to work on facing your OCD? What might you tell a friend if they were struggling with OCD? How can you be kind to yourself?

KEEP STANDING TALL, EVEN IF YOU FALL •

Yellow Flags and Warning Signs

Remember how we learned that when standing up to OCD, practice makes perfect? The same is true even after you've made great progress. For example, learning to play the piano is really hard work. Learning all those notes, then chords, then playing actual songs can take a long time and a lot of practice.

Once you've become pretty good at the piano, what would happen if you just stopped playing? What if you even went a whole six months without ever touching the piano? Would you still be just as good? Or would you be a bit out of practice?

The same is true for OCD. You've made really good progress and should be very proud. But in order to help stay that way, it's important to keep practicing. Even though you might be feeling good now, it's helpful to make a plan for what you should do if your OCD comes back. In fact, it's completely normal that OCD comes back or gets a little worse from time to time. But don't give up. The same tools you've already done such a great job learning and practicing are still helpful.

Let's look to a story about Stella.

STELLA'S STORY

Stella is eight years old and she has OCD. It's summertime and tomorrow's the first day of school. Stella has been working very hard the past few months standing up to her OCD.

Because it was summer, Stella just wanted to have fun and didn't practice her skills too much. Most of her worries have to do with her parents' safety. Before she goes to sleep, Stella used to have to ask her parents over and over again if they were "okay" and "safe." She would often use the words "make sure" or "what if" or "just in case."

Throughout the summer, Stella has been doing a great job resisting the urge to ask her parents if they were okay. But for some reason, tonight Stella feels the need to ask her parents if they're safe. She tries to fall asleep without asking, but she can't seem to get that nagging thought out of her head that something feels "wrong." Stella tries to use her skills, but she feels out of practice.

WHY IS STELLA WORRIED?

Stella should be super proud of all the hard work she's done. But for some reason, she's having trouble this time. Why might that be? Is there anything different this one night from all the other nights during summer?

Well, Stella is having her first day of school tomorrow. It's pretty normal for kids to feel different emotions about this. Some kids might be excited, and some kids might be nervous. Most kids feel a little bit of both. Also, kids usually go to bed earlier on school nights than summer nights. So, maybe Stella is struggling with her OCD this time because her routine is different. She also might be feeling nervous about the first day of school.

Finally, Stella hasn't been practicing her skills over the summer, so she might have been a little rusty when her OCD popped up!

Why Your OCD Gets Louder

Everyone is different, but there are a few common things that often make kids OCD get a little worse. These are called "yellow flags" or "warning signs." These are tiny hints that your OCD might be coming back, meaning you may need a tune-up.

Change: This is when your normal routine is mixed up. This could be anything like having a grandparent move in, changing friends, going back to school, or moving schools or houses.

New things: This could be anything like starting a new school, trying out for a sport, or going somewhere you've never been before.

Stress: This could be anything like having an argument with a friend, having a lot of homework, getting a bad grade on a test, or being picked on at school.

One more way to keep track of progress is to look at if any of these things have changed:

Duration: This means how long. For example, how long a scary thought lasts or how long you get "stuck" on something OCD tells you do to.

Frequency: This means how often. For example, how many obsessions pop into your head or how many times you need to check, repeat, count, or wash.

Intensity: This means how strong. For example, how much it bothers you to have a certain thought pop into your head or how difficult it is to stop doing something OCD tells you to do.

If these three things are decreasing, that means you're making progress. If these three things are increasing, it might mean your OCD is getting a little worse. No need to worry. This just means it's time to get back into a routine of practicing using your tools, like "The Thought Changer," "The Observer," and "Test It Out."

SPOTTING YOUR WARNING SIGNS

Below is a long, winding road. See how along the way there are some warning signs, like a triangle or a rectangle? In these empty spaces, write or draw in some things that might tell you your OCD is starting to come back. Hint: Remember your OCD detective skills!

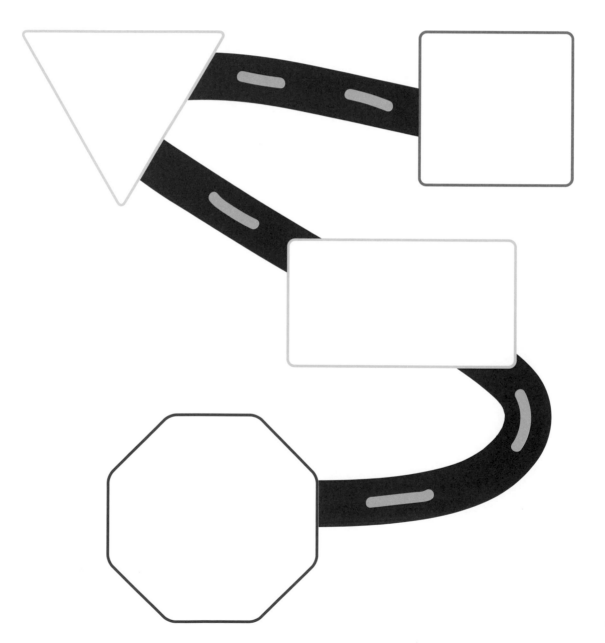

What to Do When OCD Pops Up

Sometimes OCD can be very sneaky. You may notice that as you see progress, new obsessions or compulsions pop up. This can be really frustrating! But the good news is that you can use the same skills you've already practiced and done so well with.

Let's look to a story about Dwayne.

DWAYNE'S STORY

Dwayne is 11 years old with OCD. His OCD often makes scary and unwanted thoughts jump into his head. Many of these thoughts have to do with worries about bad things happening to him, like being dirty or getting hurt.

But Dwayne has been practicing really hard standing up to his OCD. Many of the thoughts that he used to have don't pop into his head anymore, and even when some do, he doesn't get nearly as worried.

One day, Dwayne has a thought that his mother might get hurt. This is odd for Dwayne because he's never had thoughts like that before. For Dwayne, his OCD only made him have worries about bad things happening to him, but never bad things happening to others.

At first, Dwayne gets a little anxious, but he stands up to this part of his OCD just like he did with the others. Dwayne recognizes that it's just a thought. He uses the "Observer" tool and is able to just let his thought be a thought.

FEELING LIKE DWAYNE

Do you ever have times you feel like Dwayne? He has strange and scary thoughts come into his mind out of nowhere. But this time, the thoughts are different. They're about something bad happening to other people, not himself. Even though this is a little different from thoughts he's used to having, Dwayne is able to recognize that this is still his OCD talking. He doesn't panic and think that he's back at square one. Instead, he uses the same skills he's already had success with in the past. Good job, Dwayne.

CREATE A TOOLBOX COLLAGE!

You've gathered a lot of tools in your OCD toolbox. Now you need a way to remember what all those tools are. A collage full of pictures can help remind you.

For each tool you've learned about, draw a picture that makes you think of the tool. For example, for the "Observer" tool, you could draw a picture of a big pair of eyes or a pair of glasses. For "Test It Out," you could draw a picture of a scientist in a white coat. You could also draw an anchor to remind you to "stay anchored" in the present moment. What you draw is up to you.

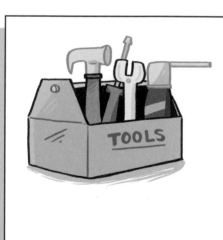

PLAYING WHACK-A-MONSTER

Below are some monsters and holes. See how some holes have monsters popping out of them and others don't? Under the empty holes, write down some of the obsessions and compulsions you've done a great job standing up to.

Under the monsters jumping out of their holes, write down any new obsessions and compulsions you might have. Maybe they're new thoughts that have started popping into your head or new actions that you have started to repeat.

Now notice the big mallet right above those monsters. Next to the mallet, write or draw in the tools you could use to stand up to your OCD. Ready, set, whack-a-monster!

Keep Standing Tall!

Excellent job. You've been working very hard and learned so much about your OCD. In fact, no one knows more about your OCD than you. You've become an expert OCD detective. You've learned many tips and tricks to show OCD who's boss. You've also added even more tools to your toolbox to help with problems beyond OCD, like thinking more balanced, being kind to yourself, and learning ways to relax your body.

Having OCD can be really difficult, but you can do this. Remember, practice makes perfect. You now have a full box of tools. If there are times when OCD is challenging, don't give up. Be sure to open up that toolbox. Keep working hard. Keep practicing. There is nothing wrong with you. Be kind to yourself. Be brave. And most importantly, keep standing tall!

RESOURCES

WEBSITES

International OCD Foundation
https://kids.iocdf.org

Anxiety and Depression Association of America
https://www.adaa.org/understanding-anxiety/obsessive-compulsive
-disorder-ocd

The National Institute of Mental Health (NIMH)
https://www.nimh.nih.gov/health/topics/obsessive-compulsive
-disorder-ocd/index.shtml

National Alliance on Mental Illness
https://www.nami.org/Learn-More/Mental-Health-Conditions
/Obsessive-Compulsive-Disorder

Centers for Disease Control and Prevention
https://www.cdc.gov/childrensmentalhealth/ocd.html

The Association for Behavioral and Cognitive Therapies (ABCT)
http://www.abct.org

Beck Institute for Cognitive Behavior Therapy
https://www.beckinstitute.org

Children and Adults with Attention-Deficit/Hyperactivity Disorder (CHADD)
https://www.chadd.org

Tourette Association of America
https://www.tourette.org

The TLC Foundation for Body-Focused Repetitive Behaviors
https://www.bfrb.org

American Academy of Child and Adolescent Psychiatry
http://www.aacap.org

Houston Area Behavioral Institute for Tourette
http://www.habitclinic.com

Psychology Houston, PC: The Center for Cognitive Behavioral Treatment
http://www.psychologyhoustonpc.com

BOOKS

Chansky, Tamar E. *Freeing Your Child from Obsessive-Compulsive Disorder: A Powerful, Practical Program for Parents of Children and Adolescents*. New York: Harmony, 2001.

Huebner, Dawn. *What to Do When Your Brain Gets Stuck: A Kid's Guide to Overcoming OCD*. Washington, DC: Magination Press, 2007.

Wagner, Aureen Pinto. *Up and Down the Worry Hill: A Children's Book about Obsessive-Compulsive Disorder and Its Treatment*. Apex, NC: Lighthouse Press, 2004.

REFERENCES

Burns, David D. *The Feeling Good Handbook: Using the New Mood Therapy in Everyday Life.* New York: Morrow, 1989.

Foa, Edna B., Coles, Meredith, Huppert, Jonathan D., Pasupuleti, Radhika V., Franklin, Martin E., and March, John. "Development and Validation of a Child Version of the Obsessive Compulsive Inventory." *Behavior Therapy* 41, no. 1 (March 2010): 121–132. doi:10.1016/j .beth.2009.02.001.

INDEX

ACKNOWLEDGMENTS

This book would not have been possible without the support and clinical insight from all the psychologists at our group practice, Psychology Houston, PC. A special thank you to Dr. Hannah Garza, Dr. Suzanne Mouton-Odum, Dr. Rosie Lasiter, and Dr. Kimberley Stanton for your contributions. Your feedback was instrumental in making the content accessible for children without compromising adherence to evidence-based practice. I'd also like to thank Katie Parr for approaching me for this project, as well as Daniel Grogan, Sean Newcott, Erik Jacobsen, Josh Moore, and the entire team at Callisto for your prompt edits and all-around helpfulness. My sincerest thanks to Emilio Salazar for your positivity, encouragement, and motivation. Writing an entire book in such a short timeframe is no easy task, so thank you for providing support, instilling confidence, and reminding me why this topic is so important to me in the first place.

ABOUT THE AUTHOR

 **Dr. Tyson Reuter** is a licensed psychologist who provides empirically supported treatments for anxiety disorders, obsessive-compulsive disorder (OCD), panic, tic disorders, and body-focused repetitive behaviors (e.g. hair pulling, skin picking). He received his doctor of philosophy in clinical psychology from the University of Houston and completed his residency in clinical psychology at Northwestern University, Feinberg School of Medicine. Dr. Reuter is a clinical assistant professor at University of Texas Medical Branch, president of the Houston Psychological Association, and cofounder of the Houston Area Behavioral Institute for Tourette (HABIT Clinic). Dr. Reuter works with patients across the developmental lifespan (childhood through adulthood), and has interest and expertise in OCD, adolescence, anxiety, tic disorders, and LGBT health. He specializes in providing solution-focused, evidence-based treatments, primarily cognitive-behavioral therapy (CBT), and has enjoyed working in a variety of treatment settings including hospitals, medical schools, inpatient psychiatric facilities, community clinics, and private practice. Dr. Reuter is trained as a scientist-practitioner and is published widely in top peer-reviewed scientific journals on various health behaviors in youth. He continues to present at national conferences and his work has been featured on major media outlets such as CNN, *USA Today*, *Newsweek*, and *U.S. News and World Report*.